A MIND APART

SUSANNE ANTONETTA

A MIND APART

Travels in a
Neurodiverse World

JEREMY P. TARCHER/PENGUIN
a member of Penguin Group (USA) Inc.   New York

JEREMY P. TARCHER / PENGUIN
Published by the Penguin Group
Penguin Group (USA) Inc., 375 Hudson Street, New York, New York 10014, USA •
Penguin Group (Canada), 90 Eglinton Avenue East, Suite 700, Toronto, Ontario M4P 2Y3,
Canada (a division of Pearson Penguin Canada Inc.) • Penguin Books Ltd, 80 Strand, London
WC2R 0RL, England • Penguin Ireland, 25 St Stephen's Green, Dublin 2, Ireland (a division of
Penguin Books Ltd) • Penguin Group (Australia), 250 Camberwell Road, Camberwell, Victoria
3124, Australia (a division of Pearson Australia Group Pty Ltd) • Penguin Books India Pvt Ltd,
11 Community Centre, Panchsheel Park, New Delhi–110 017, India • Penguin Group (NZ),
67 Apollo Drive, Rosedale, North Shore 0745, Auckland, New Zealand (a division of
Pearson New Zealand Ltd) • Penguin Books (South Africa) (Pty) Ltd, 24 Sturdee Avenue,
Rosebank, Johannesburg 2196, South Africa

Penguin Books Ltd, Registered Offices:
80 Strand, London WC2R 0RL, England

First trade paperback edition 2007
Copyright © 2005 by Suzanne Paola

Most Tarcher/Penguin books are available at special quantity discounts for bulk purchase for sales
promotions, premiums, fund-raising, and educational needs. Special books or book excerpts also
can be created to fit specific needs. For details, write Penguin Group (USA) Inc. Special Markets,
375 Hudson Street, New York, NY 10014.

The Library of Congress catalogued the hardcover edition as follows:
Antonetta, Susanne, date.
A mind apart: travels in a neurodiverse world/Susanne Antonetta.
p.   cm.
ISBN 1-58542-382-3
1. Psychology, Pathological.   I. Title.
RC454.A429   2005   2005050654
616.89—dc22

ISBN 978-1-58542-518-1 (paperback edition)

Printed in the United States of America
1   3   5   7   9   10   8   6   4   2

Book design by Kate Nichols

For Bruce and Jin, neurodivine

CONTENTS

How many ways, on how many levels, do we
discover the inaccessibility of another mind?

—Czeslaw Milosz
The Land of Ulro

What a piece of work is a man,
How noble in reason . . .

—William Shakespeare
Hamlet

A MIND APART

PROLOGUE

I AM ASKED, What is this book. And I want to say, Books are like children. They are what they are because they are not something else.

But children have their genesis—moments of love, insight, passion, transgression—and so do books. When I first came across the concept of neurodiversity, I felt a thrill of recognition: I found the term in a quote from autistic Temple Grandin, used to mean people hardwired to think differently from the norm. I have manic-depressive disorder, and one of the major changes my life has charted has been, oddly enough, just having people I can *talk to*. Really talk. Of the people I'm closest to, at a little past the midpoint of my life, one has the form of autism known as Asperger's syndrome. One has multiple personalities, and sends me messages like *I am Peggy's sister. I have a million secrets. Will you be my friend?*

Dawn, the friend with Asperger's, found human society difficult until learning to exist with gorillas, whom she got to know by falling in love with them, taking a small zoo job, and going on to become a primatologist. Her first sense of the magic of connection came when a gorilla touched her on the finger.

I e-mail N'Lili—who's a many-head, or man with different people inside him—up to three or four times a day. They are married to my cousin. I write them separately and together: in response they might say THIS IS US or THIS IS VICKI or ANNIE ASKED ME TO ASK YOU SOMETHING LOVE PEG. WE ARE CHILDREN, they say, though they live in an adult male body.

Even those I meet who don't have a syndrome you could find in the DSM-IV, the manual doctors use to assign disorders of the mind, reveal to me inner lives of honeycomb intricacy, bitterness and sweetness: judges' chambers, elevators inside. Animals, the more we insert ourselves into their consciousnesses, reflect back startling strangenesses and familiarities: song as language, painting as personal expression. This is a book about different kinds of minds.

LAST WEEK for two days I couldn't read: I ended up holding books in front of my face as if they were fans. I wanted to read, and my books had charm for me, but the words slid off the page or stuck, gnarls in a river. I couldn't read because I had word aversions, to several words I can't type even now or think about, unless in my mind I scramble them. One is a word that appears in recipes, so I couldn't read recipes or look at cookbooks. The aversion seemed to stem from two consonants in a certain order.

Come to think of it, I also couldn't read because of word infatu-ations: when my eye got to certain words I love—*smooth* and *lush,* for instance—I would have to slow and caress them. After a while I realized my eye wasn't going anywhere but stayed stuck, like a needle in a groove. There it is. Here I jog it along.

Anyway, I have bipolar disorder and have to tolerate lots of odd, unruly things happening in my head. The reading problem got so annoying I wrote to my friend Dawn. I wondered if she ever felt the same thing, and she wrote back,

> Virtually every word I hear or see is onomatopoetic (sp?) to me. I can't stand the word *stimulation* (and it is even worse when e-mail groups shorten it, as many of my autistic ac-quaintances do, to "stim." AAHHHHHH!!!!!) It's like nails on a chalkboard—it even makes my face hurt. Probably be-cause it forms a feedback loop in my brain and becomes what the word describes. Luckily, I have words like *cream* and *foam* to balm the ache.

We talk like this a lot. Do you feel the number five is brown? Can you hold it when it comes to you, unassuming in its brown-ness? How does everyone resist the lusciousness of others' minds, moving around us, with us, all the time, like a gallery of veiled art?

> *Not in itself indeed; it is a trifle unworthy your exalted rank. . . . But on account of the author, who is the first being of the kind, and yet without a name.*
>
> *He was once a man.*

Simon Brown, a clergyman, described himself this way in a letter to Queen Caroline of England. He dedicated his defense of Christianity to her. The *Defense* became a widely loved work, though at the time he wrote it, the author claimed his soul had been sucked from his body, leaving him a brute or a husk.

IN A RECENT BACK ISSUE of *The Atlantic* I found an article titled "Neurodiversity." Not only was the subject there but the piece was dated the date after my birthday, which, possibly because of my neurodiverse way of thinking, led me to attach all kinds of importance to it. A short piece, it brought together two other pieces of writing—Jon Katz's "GeekForce" columns in the e-zine *HotWired,* and a website called the Institute for the Study of the Neurologically Typical. The site borrows the language of autism literature, offering diagnostic screenings for neurotypicality, online "papers," and diagnostic criteria like "Neurotypical syndrome is a neurobiological disorder characterized by preoccupation with social concerns, delusions of superiority, and obsession with conformity."

Katz's "GeekForce" columns, on the rise of geekdom as an "epic" social movement, don't mention the neuroatypical, but Katz discusses the geeks in the computer age as the socially clueless become cool, and the author of the *Atlantic* article, Harvey Blume, refers readers to the Institute site if they want to understand the "possible neurological underpinnings of GeekForce." One of the site creator's "symptoms" of neurotypicality is technology trouble. Often, nonautistics see wholes; autistics are more likely to see parts, which can make them more adept with computers. The Comments section of the Institute website, in between speculations that neuroatypicals may be the next step in human evolution, includes lots of vents at the neurotypical's fumbling around with computers or VCRs.

"In other words, NT is only one kind of brain wiring," Blume writes, "and, when it comes to working with hi-tech, quite possibly an inferior one."

The common assumption in cognitive studies these days is that the human brain is the most complicated two-and-a-half pounds of matter in the known universe. With so much going on in a brain, the argument goes, the occasional bug is inevitable: hence autism and other departures from the neurological norm. ISNT [the Institute] suggests another way of looking at this. Neurodiversity may be every bit as crucial for the human race as biodiversity is for life in general. Who can say what form of life may prove best at any given moment?

Another cyberphilosopher, Kate Hayles, comments to me that "the most powerful competitors now for the niche humans occupy [on the planet] are intelligent machines." They, not lions and tigers, are the ones we need to worry about in the twenty-first century.

HOW AMAZING, how twenty-first-century, perhaps: the fact that we have each other, Dawn and me, that we can talk to groups of people like ourselves who come together, often in cyberspace, the fact that we exist at all in these ways and these numbers, when one hundred years ago we might have been in the type of perpetual confinement called the "rest cure" or, a few hundred years before that, treated with whips.

That fact that we have words like *neurotypicals* (or *normies*, or *NTs*) and *neuroatypicals* and *Aspies* (people with Asperger's) and *ACs* (Autistics and Cousins) and *van Gogh's disease* (bipolar disorder). We talk about communicating *cross-culturally* with *NTs*. And there are more of us: more people with autism, anxiety, depression, attention-deficit problems.

Some say our society is practicing *unnatural selection*. Unlike Darwinian selection, where the strong and the adept survive, now the weak thrive and do better, according to this theory. We make the weak, through toxins in the environment, through stress. We coddle them with treatment and social services. Smart, sturdy, naturally selected people use birth control and take trips to the Himalayas instead of making babies together.

By some estimates, within four years one in one hundred Americans will have autism. Bipolar disorder in adults seems stable at 1 to 2 percent of the population, but it has suddenly begun to appear in young children. (An extensive *Time* magazine article on this subject in 2002 drew no conclusions on whether the disease, formerly "the rare province of luckless adults," was increasing in our young or simply being diagnosed at younger ages.) There's the rise of ADHD, and other syndromes like Tourette's.

I believe that all selection, however it occurs, is natural, and only the future can tell what selection will bear fruit. (And what fruit may ultimately turn to poison: the intellect that can plan the hunt precedes the concept of fission; the restless flexible fore-finger precedes the gun.)

THE EVOLUTION of the neurodiverse into community and communities has happened partly through numbers and partly through the World Wide Web. For many of us, the difficulty of finding other people who share our mind ways and communication styles and the discomfort of having to provide immediate answers or, perhaps, account for bodies and eye contact in conversation makes the Web a preferred way to speak. And appropriately, the Web drew a great deal of inspiration from an information system called Xanadu, developed by a hyperactive adult named Ted Nelson. Nelson coined the term *hypertext* and conceptualized a universe of linked information; he speaks happily of his mind: "Attention Deficit Disorder was coined by regularity chauvinists," he remarked to a reporter from *Wired* magazine. "Regularity chauvinists are people who insist that you have got to do the same thing every time, every day, which drives some of us nuts. Attention Deficit Disorder—we need a more positive term for that. *Hummingbird mind*, I should think." Hummingbird mind, presumably, because with attention deficit the mind hovers and darts among many, many things, never entirely planting itself.

KATHLEEN SEIDEL runs an enormous website, largely devoted to autism, called Neurodiversity.com. She and I have been conversing on and off in cyberspace. She sends me, one day, an article about a presentation made by Boyd Haley, chairman of the

chemistry department at the University of Kentucky, a man rant-
ing about how the United States spent millions investigating one
mad cow from Canada, while ignoring what he calls "mad child disease": "attention deficit disorder, autism, autism spectrum disorder, or pervasive development disorder." He attributes mad child
disease—a "major disaster," he terms it—to mercury toxicity.

I'm interested in the theory of mercury toxicity, whether it's
true we're poisoning our children the way we flush poisons into
fish and mammals in the sea. But to think of children as those
downer cattle, struggling on their legs and unable even to be use-
fully slaughtered.

Kathleen's website is subtitled "Honoring the Diversity of
Human Wiring." The gateway screen shows the faces of philoso-
pher Ludwig Wittgenstein, mathematician Alan Turing, artist
Andy Warhol, pianist Glenn Gould, all believed to be autistic.

Many things regarded as pathologies can be terrible, rendering
a life as most people would define it—with things like autonomy
and connection—impossible. Those lives are not the ones I'm covering here in this book. In many cases, though, things regarded as
pathologies come with tremendous abilities, whatever behavior
those gifts might come calling in. The *Wired* reporter notes that Ted
Nelson drove like a maniac and wore a belt made of dog collars.

MANIC-DEPRESSIVES tend to have a connection with creativity, a link studied from the time of Aristotle on. Psychiatrist Kay
Redfield Jamison, herself manic-depressive, probed this connection in *Touched with Fire* and takes it back to Dionysius, a god afflicted with cyclical madness who bestowed the gift of creativity.

Colors "leap out" or become more themselves for us—"redder reds, greener greens," as one bipolar puts it. Words move. The painter van Gogh was bipolar, as were Virginia Woolf, Georgia O'Keeffe, Sylvia Plath, Gerard Manley Hopkins, Gioacchino Rossini, and hundreds of other artists.

"I feel like Rossini makes *me* manic," says my brother, Chris, when we listen to *The Barber of Seville*.

OF THE PEOPLE I KNOW who qualify as neuroatypical, including myself, I do not know any who refuse medication or therapy. (There are enormous questions, too, about the balance of patient control versus physician control of the therapeutic process, and overmedication. These would take books to address, so I won't be taking them on here.) I take medication and have for some thirty years. I have three tan vials, three neurocorrectors— primarily a drug called Depakote—that tether me to your world wholly, if you live on the other side of this divide. When prescriptions run out or I misplace hand luggage, the panic's overwhelming, childlike. I have no desire to develop more word infatuations and word aversions, and more of other things as well.

But with the challenges come the gifts. And the sense, often raised by my correspondents, that the word *cure* is the wrong word, and that we must begin to respect the mental processes of the individual, think in terms of helping to get the gifts to emerge while the challenges become as manageable as they can. We need to develop new terms of value and of tolerance, especially as medical work in the alteration of the gene makes possible the eradication of our kind.

Kathleen Seidel writes to the Congressional Autism Caucus,

[M]any autistic adults have described how they find eye contact uncomfortable, distressing and counterproductive to comprehension or communication; many have described how rocking or other harmless repetitive acts help to calm their nerves and focus on matters at hand. I believe that we should pay attention to such information so that we do not end up spending a lot of time and effort trying to persuade both autistic children and adults to imitate behavior that is alien and nonfunctional to them, or to eradicate behavior that is natural and useful to them, for the sole purpose of making it easier for inflexible neurologically typical people to feel comfortable in their presence.

Temple Grandin has said of the possibility of genetic engineering, "Civilization would probably pay a terrible price if the genes that cause autism and Asperger's syndrome were eradicated. The world might become a place full of highly social yakkity-yaks who would never do anything new or creative."

I don't believe the world could become a place of highly social yakkity-yaks. But it also frightens me, the easy possibility of erasure of my own way of thinking.

MY VAN GOGH'S DISEASE has a place in the world, but as long as I've been aware of what's come to be called neurodiversity in my own thinking—which in some form I think I have been all my life—I have come with wonder to the whole question of consciousness. If other people don't have word aversions, how do they feel what they read? How do they think?

When I was fourteen, I wrote in my diary, "I feel so absolutely hollow, like someone carved me out like a pumpkin." I wrote this a month or so after a stab at suicide landed me unconscious for three days in a hospital: a light rain of saline washed a bottle of Quaaludes from my blood. I noted this event, too, in my diary: "tried to kill myself, was saved (obviously)." In a few more weeks, though, I'm writing, "I'm in such a good mood. I can't wait till tomorrow." Every possibility seemed to float in my personal ether and land randomly on my mind and body. I wrote and composed music and painted and experimented. I imagined conspiracies and addressed myself by several different names.

Homo sum, wrote the Roman playwright Terence: I am human. Nothing human is foreign to me.

I FIRST BEGAN TRACKING what felt to me like the difference of my own thoughts around the age of eleven. At the time, as I recorded my conscious experiences, I did so with shame and terror. Therefore my astonishment at the world I've grown into, of Dawn, N'Lili, of whole cybercommunities coming together for the purpose of defining who we are and what we want from medical treatment. It is a brave new world, in which I can easily find other people to talk over the same questions with, to say, Do you ever find you can't read because a certain word repels you, like the wrong pole of a magnet? It's a world that offers enough wonder, in itself and in the discussions it creates—of gifts and challenges, of all that comes with neurodiversity—to make me want to sit down with it, and consider it from as many places as possible (and this is just a start; there are infinite places to look), to think hard about this defining aspect of my life, and the lives of others around me.

I would not have the hubris to declare anyone else's life livable for them. I write for myself and for those who do find a value, even a rich existence, in their mind ways, modified perhaps by treatment, but resonant still of what they are.

In these meditations I have looked at my own bipolar disorder and other neuroatypical ways of being; the concept of consciousness and language in animals, who also have their gifts; and to lay a framework for the questions raised by neuroatypical consciousness, I delve a bit into the relatively modern world of consciousness studies and the ongoing world of theories of evolution, which always deal largely with the evolution of that seemingly wondrous thing, the human mind. I see my son's consciousness developing; I face the minds of those who are, by human standards, monstrous, mentally wired in a way we can't begin to understand. There are many voices in this book. Some belong to friends and family, some are those who have helped me along, answered questions for me, or simply served as other examples of different and viable ways to live a human life. Some, like Shakespeare and Augustine, provide a dialogue, with those who have faced some fairly fundamental human questions.

MY HUSBAND, BRUCE, reads this and says, Tell them it's a bipolar book.

Hey, out there. It's a bipolar book.

Though I, too, have to ask him what that means. He says, alinear, associational: I always have many things happening in my mind at once. To be honest, I am some of the many voices in this book.

And you, reader, the mirror, as Baudelaire wrote, the veiled jury. I must account for you.

THE HUMAN ROAD

IT IS SPRING NOW, and a pod of five gray whales swims into our harbor in Bellingham Bay, a detour in their annual Alaska migration. Our bay is polluted with mercury and chlorine from a Georgia-Pacific plant, which produces toilet paper, treating the paper with chlorine to make it whiter. The plant sends a nonstop cumulus of chemical-smelling steam into the air, like it's manufacturing another brand of sky. I accept the plant as part of the landscape, like the Northwest's chronic real clouds, and in my acceptance I find another kind of betrayal.

Like most polluted bays, our Bellingham Bay makes rich and luxuriant flora, a soup of algae, drawing in the hungry whales.

I take my son, Jin, to a park that crescents along the water, to watch them. He's close to three and I keep thinking about his developing memory. My earliest memories are from his age. Only some 20,000 gray whales remain on the earth, no longer a small enough number to be called endangered, but not too many more than my university has staff and students. Who knows what will become of the grays? They, and the orcas here, seem to be losing the ability to reproduce. They suffer from *encroachment*, from *viability issues*.

The whales are strips of black rubber separating the water now and then: moving spumes. When they surface and blow, the crowd claps. A young girl in jeans has climbed onto a boulder and dances there, a slow, undulating, arm-waving feet-on-the-ground dance, a Northwest expression of ecstasy. A businessman in a navy suit holds binoculars to his eyes and a cell-phone to his ear. I see women in suits and heels, tie-dyed kids from local communes. Everybody's here.

"Watch this," I say to Jin, "remember this," over and over, because the whales are too theoretical for him, refusing to carry their bodies where we can see them clearly; Jin chases the dirty-looking gray gulls that march full-on in front of us. I want him to record the whales for the future, like a human videotape. His lens takes in other images: women in Indian-print dresses beat drums; a young man with blond dreadlocks writhes in front of them, another dancer. They stare out at the whales, except for the dancer, who just circles regularly toward the mammals, flailing his arms in invitation. When people approach the women to ask what they're doing, they say the whales are spirit guides, like angels, who come to humans to teach them to live at a higher level of spiritual evolution.

The human outlines on my Honda's dashboard—reclining, with sketchy lines to show air blowing to the head, the torso, or the feet—Jin has come to call "angels." I don't have a clue where he learned the word. "Turn on angels," he says, when he wants to press the buttons.

WHALES HAVE FOLLOWED a different evolutionary path from ours, beginning on land and then becoming, in the water, one of the great predators of the Eocene—archeocetes, huge crocodile-y monsters with gaping teeth—before mellowing into these toothless mammals that live in social groups and nurture their young. Gray whales are a baleen whale, a simple class of whales also called "mysticetes." They feed through baleen plates, spongy scrims in the mouth that suck seawater and let in the tiny organisms they eat—porcelain crab larvae, ghost shrimp. Like all whales, grays are mammals and intelligent, large-brained, with a much larger brain than ours (a fact I suspect the whale drummers would tell me lots about if I asked them), but compared with other whales they're relatively slow in evolving, having lived in their present form for some 12 million years, leaving their Eocene form 20 million years before that. Using baleen is a peaceful way to feed, compared with other members of the whale family, who might stun prey such as schools of mackerel with sound waves, dive, and eat.

When the whales surface you can see, with binoculars, the crust of thousands of barnacles on their backs, the quick dives of birds that live off the smaller lives whales carry, kelp and bladderwort tangles on their flukes. They're like islands, or planets, so whole and different they absorb our projections the way stars do: some people I know in Bellingham say whales are aliens from other worlds, come to teach us how to evolve so we can join with them. The spaceships they see hovering over us travel to contact the whales, besides doing other things, like abducting people. A hairdresser I know tells all her clients about her own abduction.

A grueling exerience, she says. "But they won't come for you," she adds, parting hair, "unless you're spiritually ready."

AT NOON ONE DAY, I walk across the campus where I work. It is, you have to understand, 1999, and we're all feeling a bit twitchy. If you have not visited this place in time, as I have, I need to tell you a computer glitch called Y2K is supposed to crash everything at the turn of the millennium, as computers read the new zeros as meaning 1900. Crash predictions range from a few power and phone outages to the end of the world as we know it, and folks, as they do on these occasions, stock up on water. A preacher, who visits our campus every year and calls himself Bible Tom, turns on me from his small group of listeners. The crowd of students looks mostly amused, using Tom to punctuate their swallows of Starbucks. Tom is middle-aged, hard-looking, his face like a callus with features—a callus on the open hand of a God about to smite.

"You might think you're a good person!" he yells at me. "Your friends and family might think you are a good person. To God you are not a good person. To God you are an evil, rebellious wretch."

All around us—me, Bible Tom, the few students milling about—the spruce and hemlock and long-armed cedars wave their limbs like many-armed Hindu gods. Ours is a maritime climate; there's always a good wind here. It's spring, around Easter time, when Bible Tom comes back with the robins and the Canada geese.

This campus is red. Redbrick buildings with tall windows rounded at the top, coaxed ivy: the self-conscious college. When I see the buildings, they stand both as they are, in the blush of warm spring rain, and as they might be dug out in a few millennia, caked, crumbled, in a tilth of rubble, compacted volcanic ash. I don't want to see this way: it's like a sickness. It is manic of me, I suppose, to have to see so many ways at once; yet part of what the turn of the millennium brings with it is a sense of the world as manic. To Tom I walk across campus like an embodiment of humanity's fall. What am I wearing? I don't mark that in my notebook.

How do you know? I imagine myself saying to Bible Tom. How do you know I'm not saved?

Or maybe, How do you know so much about me? I am pulling the world apart, brick by brick, with my mind. And meanwhile, at the omniplex, in a rush of millennial movies, Arnold Schwarzenegger fights the devil, handsome Gabriel Byrne, with the help of some really, really big guns in *End of Days*. He hardly bothers calling on God at all, and though Byrne at one point manages to crucify him, Arnold escapes.

GRAYS IN THE PACIFIC migrate 10,000 miles a year, from the Bering Sea down to Mexico, where they calve and hunger for the cold. The only other gray whale migration route is along the Korean peninsula; grays used to migrate the Atlantic but were hunted to extinction there. Only a few hundred still swim along the coast of Korea, but I like thinking how my son, not yet three and born in Seoul, has lived along both their habitats. Ours is a gray, corrugated water—it wears the tint of its cold heart—lined with the tall sparse cones of Sitka spruce. I can't guess at the look of the far-off waters of Korea.

"Say hello to the whales!" I say. "Some whales like this live in Korea, like you did." Jin looks at me with that incredulous look kids develop a few months out of babyhood, when they're already beyond a parent's bright, optimistic inanities.

When Jin was adopted and arrived here, five months old, he cried at night, for hours. Still thinking it was daytime and grieving Korea, other seas, other bodies moving through the darkness. It was November, the time of year when the wind rips off the bay, the house rocks, and wisteria whips the windows—when the wind lets us know it's been harboring all year a kind of killer rage. I walked and rocked Jin. I hummed melodies that went on and on and ended nowhere. I sang him, only because they were the songs I knew, old English folk tunes where lovers drowned or died by the sword, ships were wrecked, Lord Franklin sought a passage around the Pole and never came back. It was throat-scraping work. Some nights it took twenty or thirty tragedies to calm him down.

It seemed like an awful thing to do to a baby, to uproot him, to scare him with such a wind. To soothe him with tragedy. Jin had a mystical beauty: round, pale cheeks, eyes so curious they drank the surfaces off things. I already loved him too much to want anyone to do to him what I had just done. How had Bible Tom known this, too?

Agency workers call it the "transition time," the "predictable grieving." Before Jin came, I willed myself not to think about this. Then it sounded in my ear, all night, as we walked: an outrage ripped from far off, like the wind's.

Now, at two and a half, Jin loves me so much he calls me *his*, swats away my husband's hands and lips.

I REMEMBER going to bed as a child and feeling emerge around me in the dark the hushed, occult world of Adult Things. Often, since my father went to night school, after I went to bed the door of our apartment would open and he would come home. I don't have specific memories of that bedroom I shared with my brother, but I do have the sense of a curtain of dark, softened by the weak bulb of a nightlight, that fell like a theater curtain, to close on my daytime act of Barbies and Velveeta and Bullwinkle and open on my parents' nighttime—an adult act full of drama and nuance I wasn't allowed to watch. I heard whispers and the whisk of curbed, careful movements. Voices fell from their normal low level—we lived in close quarters—when my parents hit on something they didn't want us to hear. Or that's what I guessed when the conversation dipped out midsentence and then came back up in volume. This shift in my apartment to adultness obsessed me as a child, and I lay in bed imagining what I was missing, the brilliant and disturbing secrets of those whispers, the movements—furniture and dishes, scrape and clink—my parents waited all day to spring into, like this was their time to be themselves, not just the automatons who wiped noses and heated bowls of Campbell's soup. And there I was, in bed and forced to stay there.

I thought about this childhood feeling one day after Jin had finally fallen asleep. I was mashing cooked peas through the medium-fine blade of my food mill over a bowl—which never seemed to be wide enough to keep butchered peas from flying around the table—and talking to Bruce in a low voice about what Jin had eaten that day and what we thought he might eat or should eat the next. I am one of those fanatical parents—only home-cooked food, organic, full of touches like fresh tarragon in the fish I stewed for his toothless mouth. Most nights after Jin fell asleep I found myself cooking baby food in the kitchen, after picking up toys and throwing in a load of wash.

Oh, I thought over the Jackson Pollock spatter of peas, so this is what it was all along.

I AM WRITING. Jin shoves a feather under the door: a gull feather, huge, its pins tipping from white to gray. Then his two-inch, dirtmooned fingers. He doesn't want me in here, in our tiny study with the door shut, but he's learned not to open the door. "Show you something!" he croons. So clear, my weaknesses, like the blemishes on the moon: curiosity and curiosity.

THE WHALES WE GREET with writhing and ecstatic drums are starving. Under protection, the grays have repopulated, but something, possibly global warming, has killed off a lot of the small life they feed on in the Bering Sea, where they build up their fat reserves for the long migration. These whales turn off here because they can't make the final leg of their trip to Alaska. Some of them will replenish and make the last run, and others will die here, in audience to the dancers. For those, we clap and cheer their last breaths and look for them to guide us as they exhaust our small bay's food supply.

One gray, a male, dies during Holy Week. His body fascinates me, and it becomes a ritual, my daily viewing of the dead whale: there's Mass on Ash Wednesday, smudge, dead whale. First the whale corpse is a lump in the water, an island, with none of the arching muscularity of a living gray. As it gets closer to land and more exposed, the island produces a toneless fluke.

The corpse beaches gently, right at the edge of the Georgia-Pacific plant. Before the whale lands, someone sneaks into G-P and erects a wooden cross. When the corpse has drifted within a few feet of shore, the city of Bellingham wraps off the stretch of shore in crime scene tape and adds a full-time security guard, to prevent I-don't-know-what whale violations.

I have been reading about metabolism lately, the timing of our bodies—heart rate, blood flow—by which we learn to time the earth around us. Our body's speed is the clock that invents us. What's faster than our body rhythms, like a shooting star, is fast; what's slower is slow. I learn that to the whales, with their slow metabolisms, humans appear speeded-up, so the dancers greeting the whales with their swaying scooped-arm movements would have looked to the whales at sea jerky, spastic, desperately flapping.

By Holy Thursday the dead whale's reached the shore. A dog of ours has just died, a Brittany spaniel. He died, old and cancerous, at the foot of my bed, after I held him, fed him canned cat food from a spoon. In the morning Jin leaves a stuffed dog that looks just like the spaniel carelessly on the floor, in a skewed posture that mimics the dog's sprawl in death. Front legs stretched wide in a way no living animals' could, in the jelly before rigor mortis. I pick the stuffed dog up, toss it in a toy chest. Then drive to the whale, now right under the low bluff of sand and pebbles and the yellow tape. It's thirty-five feet of dark skin that looks strangely artificial, like car leather, mouth lolling to show the pleated paper of baleen. Flukes, the gross pores of barnacles. And the eye! Brainy, open, huge, a cerebral dinner plate.

As always, a few dozen people have parked here and gawk along the coast. The balding, paunched security guard is, as always, gleeful. "In a day it will stink all over Bellingham," he says cheerfully, gesturing at the whale.

In fact, the city's reeling with the problem of whale disposal. The creature weighs probably twenty tons and is largely blubber—fat's an unpretty thing when it decays—and no one here can remember dealing with this problem before. In a newspaper story a councilwoman complains that she doesn't want a "smelly whale" ruining her city. A friend named Mary tells me a town in Oregon faced the same problem and finally dynamited the creature.

"But there was a huge rain of blubber all over town for a while," she comments matter-of-factly, as if people just went inside and got out their blubber-proof coats. I try to imagine that: a self-made biblical plague.

Besides me, the most common guests to the whale are parents and children, mostly toddlers. The little ones cry to poke it, touch its glossy eye or rough fins. The mothers and fathers drag them out of the car to see, then drag them back in. A mother says one day, "Come on, honey, there's live ones this way."

In a letter to a local paper a father carries on (I wonder if I have ever seen him!) about the whale's penis. "The damn thing," he writes, should be cut off, instead of "bobbing there" where his two daughters can see it.

Another whale washes up, on the Whidbey Island yard of a bed-and-breakfast run by our former congressman Jack Metcalf, who has voted to roll back the Clean Air Act, get rid of the Clean Water Act, exempt refineries from rules governing toxic emissions, hamstring the EPA. His environmental voting record rates a 15 out of a possible 100 by the Conservation League. I wonder what he thinks, with the whale and its eye washed up into his own private existence.

The gray has an arched rostrum, or upper head, a long snout with a long, slightly upturned, ironic mouth. Its eyes stand above the end of the mouth, as if our eyes blinked out from the lower cheeks. There's a calm, mossy brainpower in whales' eyes, and this gives grays a rueful look, like they know they deserve better than just staring face-forward at their food all day. Our whale's body beaches on its side, so it stares quietly and patiently at the rain that fills its eye and runs out the corners. The eye has the quality of eyes in those trick paintings—eyes that follow you everywhere you go in the room, left, right, or middle. I feel it on me, everywhere in Bellingham.

. . .

WHAT DO THE WHALES SEE when they see us on shore? Something too quick, too nervous to be alive. Perhaps they would want to comfort us humans, though not for the reasons we imagine.

Whether they think about us, in any way we would find intelligible, is the real question that keeps us glued to the cool grass at Boulevard Park.

It feels like a lesser form of what I feel looking at my young son: the drive to know his consciousness, his growing humanness; the thoughts that are sifting in his head, always, turning dashboard figures into winged swoops of grace—or maybe to him angels are just slouched sketches of the human, supine. Where and how that happens. To know his mind. To know.

JIN HAS BEGUN asking questions, in the endless perseverant way of small children.

Why is it dark sometimes? and I tackle the earth's rotation, the question of days and nights.

Why is it *today?* and I begin again.

What is tomorrow? and again I'm talking, sorting through the facts, offering what seems plausible to him. (The earth is like a big ball and it turns around and there's the sun again.)

Why is tomorrow *tomorrow?* he says, with mounting frustration, and the questions keep coming in an infinite regress of questions, to the point where language dissolves utterly—it's clear that he's not asking about planets and turning at all—and another explanation of time will only get back a plaintive *Why is tomorrow tomorrow? Why?*

I always cheat at the end and say, Why are you you?, knowing I'm just tired and punking out, drawing a curtain over the whole problem with an unfair existential feint.

AND WHY AM I ME? And why is N'Lili N'Lili, or Dawn Dawn? Evolution, my friend Thor keeps telling me, doesn't care about perfection. But it would be strange if something like the human leg—if it were born sometimes two, sometimes eight, sometimes clawed, sometimes toed—showed the same variation as consciousness.

Whales vocalize about many things—food, danger, mating— through a system of sounds with names like *hauntings* and *trumpets*. And they click and whistle and sing, in two-tone themes that build toward nothing and sound (to us) both complex and primeval, yanked from the ocean floor. The orca pods housed in our Northwest waters have individual dialects, and one pod member takes on the job of teaching the young of the group how to vocalize. Whale species that like to sing have whales in each group, more accomplished singers, that sing more than others; the rest listen more. Performer and audience. Humpback whales have a common breeding song made up of four to ten musical themes—sequences of notes—that each singer changes so that each year the song evolves, as the males follow one another's improvisations and add their own. Speeded up a lot, the humpbacks sound like birds. Speeded up somewhat, they sound just like human music.

Scientists like the late Donald Griffin at Harvard, an animal mind theorist, call this "musical intelligence." It's a sense of language not just as survival but as an aesthetic tool, a source of pleasure, a reason to listen to a pod member who might otherwise be poaching on your turf of ghost shrimp, a reason to swim up, as they do, to human researchers blasting symphonies on underwater speakers, though they must sense by now we're their only real predator.

It may be that musical intelligence describes the minds of many humans we find as a society unintelligible. Autistics, manic-depressives, schizophrenics can think musically. We have imagined ourselves as being not just God's image but an image that replicates shiny and alike as sequins on a gown. But some of us, maybe many of us, are more like our distant cousins than like one another.

I'VE BEEN THINKING LATELY about *Devil's Advocate*, one of the movies I've watched in the millennial wave. This devil's a lawyer. He lives in a palace of dark stone and is named John Milton, after the poet. Why, I'm wondering? Is this supposed to be demonic humor, summoning up the author of *Paradise Lost*? Or a frank acknowledgment of the pious poet's fallenness, when, caught between the demands of faith (the devil as nothing) and the demands of literature (great characters), he chose the latter. It's a critical chestnut that we love Milton's devil. He has all the best language.

I ask people what they think of evil, to see how it's appeared to them: the answer always holds the idea of narrative. Lance Morrow, the author of *Evil: An Investigation*, wrote that "evil is always intimately connected with the idea of story." Language gives us so many ways to say something else entirely, things like *habitat encroachment* and *viability* and *transition* and *grieving.* Our speech is riddled with markers of its own inconsistency: *Let's say*, we say, or *Let's put it this way,* as if in speech we choose how to place the truth of an event, like a piece on a chessboard. If we found the minds that could not say *viability issues* or *collateral damage,* we might discover that we need them.

Once Dawn was at my house and we sat around a table, drinking pricey Scotch older than I am that, sadly, tasted to me like kerosene. We were talking about chimps and evil.

"Chimps can have wars. They have gang violence. They can do everything we do," Dawn said, as I got more and more burn-tongued and woozy, "except tell stories about what they do. But that's huge."

TO INDICATE A PREDATOR, the head of an orca pod, the matriarch, will utter a high-pitched whistle. If she does not achieve these tones, she says nothing at all.

To the cetacean freaks—I imagine, to those drumming women, maybe to me sometimes—whales are huge, gentle gods, consciousness without fault, language without lies. Neurodiversity dreamed to its highest point, with a consciousness streaming in rolling movements, beginnings and ends, and without language.

Hasn't it always seemed right that in the era of whaling, when our country knew whales, an ex-whaler would write *Moby-Dick*? The prey of Ahab, a man named for a wicked king in the Old Testament, could not have been an elephant or a rhino or a squid, large and even desirable as these may be. It had to be a good opponent, sentient, and intimately wrapped up in questions of good and evil. It had to be something that had been here for millions of years and was perhaps about to be here no longer, slain by an evolutionary upstart.

I AM SHAMBLING through what's left of my world—well, not the Real-I who holds the now-quaint computer mouse in her hand but the general *I* of the species. It is the italic *I*, reader, who could just as well be you, what's left of us, after the future bites off the strands of us it likes. This *I* walks through the dental geometry of foundation—tawny brick, rounded casement—the same way Real-I once walked through ruins in Rome: curious, collecting the experience, amused at the earnestness with which these people took their lives—like having special rooms for washing their bodies when their defenses against the future were, after all, so poor. Real-I would never concede to be so temporary, though she's not sure where this confidence arises—it's blood-pressure confidence, oxygen confidence, the confidence of the living in lording it over the dead. I'm sure you, too, know about this.

Maybe for this future *I* the overdeveloped Northwest has ceded itself and between the rubble old growth is here again—

Sitka spruces the size of low office towers, Douglas firs thick enough to live in, Western hemlocks with the lopsided sprigs at the top, pointing the way of the wind. Or maybe the anthropogenic world will have closed over, ponds of concrete and structure everywhere, islands of grass. The crows, who thrive on humanity, will have the numbers and stimulation to diversify as a species: the new *I* picks her way through the preserved ruins inside their titanium-alloy fence surrounded by white crows, or crows with hooked beaks for digging through pavement, or crows that sing with the voices of early robins before croaking with outrage.

Or it will be just thirty years from now, but still changed, and Jin and I, the *I* that is me, now, can stand on the shoreline again. I can show him where he once saw gray whales: where they spouted and rolled and heard the too-fast bird chirps of humans crying to them onshore. Anglo-Saxon poets once called their whale-filled Atlantic "whale-road"—that's how plentiful the mammals were—though the whales they saw, like the sperm whale, are now almost extinct, and the rolling backs of tankers have taken their place.

Perhaps in the future everyone's genes get gentled into place before birth, and no one like me or Dawn or N'Lili exists. We'll be part of another great extinction, the toppling of some more of the earth's top predators.

If we hum, we might speak with whales' voices, inventing the same pointless tunes. They are so much us they could write our songs; isn't it funny to know that, now that they're almost gone? Of course, when we talk about the grays in that future, it will depend on how we talk: *Let's put it this way—they weren't able to adapt; it's nature's way,* we could say, which is to say, *We are nature now.* Or maybe there'll still be this village-worth of them, clinging to their strip of coastline, their movement as foreordained as my son's.

Human road, we could say to all we see, Where to?

DREAMING

The human face is an empty power, a field of death. . . .
[A]fter countless thousands of years that the human face
has spoken and breathed, one still has the impression that it
hasn't even begun to say what it is and what it knows.

—ANTONIN ARTAUD

This is all a dream, isn't it?

—MY SON, JIN

MY SON SAID THIS when we returned from a trip to find
our house scrabbling with mice. By the evidence—the
soft scratchy feet in the walls and crawl space above the ceiling,
piles of caraway-seed scat on the floor—there must have been
hundreds. Savannah, my ancient cat, dragged her back legs over
to the kitchen baseboard, suddenly a froth of scratching paws,
and watched, like we'd created for her, out of a love even she
must have recognized as improbably huge, a nonstop theater.

Sometime just before that we'd all gone to see a plant called
a corpse flower, an eight-foot-tall monster of a plant from Suma-
tra that blooms just for one night every couple of years with the
odor of rotting meat. Jin called it the "stinky flower," and we
found that our clothes and our car stank for days afterward, as if
our own fleshly decay had accelerated. Anyway, that was many

showers and colognes behind us, but in the middle of the mouse incident Bruce and I woke up one morning and sat bolt upright in bed.

"It's the corpse flower."

And the smell was; we expected to find the huge pink thing, that managed to look like both a phallus and a vulva, poking up through our bedroom floor. Then we woke up fully.

"Uh-oh. The mice."

Yes, the mice. Under the fridge, three little corpses. They had had no odor and then overnight begun smelling like death itself. We tilted the refrigerator over, and Bruce picked them out with butter knives and pliers; the little bodies had gone flat, sticky. They puffed away in a cloud of vile gas. At this point my young son decided we must all be dreaming.

SO I AM GOING to start by going back to something I'm not at all sure about, a dim memory, not much different from a dream. At fifteen my parents took me to a psychiatrist who declared me schizophrenic and told them they couldn't expect anything from me except maybe a lifetime of institutions. I don't remember much about this guy, Dr. L. He was short, middle-aged, morose, with a face like a wrinkled olive, and I remember thinking even then that he didn't seem to talk to me much, which led me to wonder how he reached his conclusions. I think he occasionally bit off a morose question and I probably squirmed, in my teenage and bipolar angst, rather than answer it. And so I ended up a hopeless schizophrenic. I had and still have some weird affects, but if he'd chosen to talk to me he would have discovered my touch with reality was fine, relatively. If memory serves, we mostly sat and stared at each other, like we were some new postverbal species aborning, and so I got diagnosed.

This happened so long ago I can't find him or confirm any of this. It comes back to me, in a flood dreamlike in its imprecision, when I decide to attend the trial of Kyle Anderson, a teenage neighbor who killed a little boy about a mile from my house this past spring. Both boys lived four blocks away from us. Eight-year-old Thomas, tied with duct tape, choked, mutilated by sixteen-year-old Kyle because he had "pestered" Kyle with questions about a fishpond. Kyle led him to an overgrown concrete works heavy with trees and grasses, promising a game.

When I saw the boys' pictures on the news, I recognized them right away, oddly similar and familiar in their linen-pale hair and slightly pug noses. The victim Thomas groomed in a crew cut and a photographer's smile, Kyle smirking and disheveled. I've seen both swinging feet first in the air. They're just neighborhood boys.

The decision to attend the trial is itself dreamlike; I only go to the courtroom midway through the trial to hear an hour or so of testimony, and then, in a compulsion that feels migratory or enforced, wake up every morning and head there, go back unthinkingly in the afternoon, change child care plans, cancel a class to hear closing arguments.

A LOT HAS BEEN DECIDED before this trial. The defense has admitted Kyle committed the murder: Kyle's on his second defense team, and with his first he lost his right to be tried as a juvenile, so he's standing trial as an adult. All this we know: Kyle lured the child to a brushy field with the promise of a game, duct-taped his hands behind his back and his mouth, apparently as part of the game (though he never taped the boy's legs; at that point the child may have begun to struggle). Kyle had behavioral problems and took ADHD medication, sometimes withheld from him by his fundamentalist Christian mother on religious grounds.

The lawyers come to argue how the crime should be interpreted and punished; they come to debate Kyle's mind. The victim's family comes for what I hear a grandmother call "our justice." I come partly to see if Kyle, this threat to my peace, will be locked away from my family forever, and partly for reasons I can't articulate. As in, I once had a dream my family—mother and father and brother—went past me on a conveyor belt, in pieces; some force bent me down, held me there, to look.

THE COURTROOM when I enter it feels tiny, much smaller than I imagined, and like a church, two rows of four wood pews. It looks much more like a church than my Jerusalem Orthodox church, which meets at a funeral home and looks just like what it is, a warehouse for the dead. People coming in to the courtroom seat themselves carefully, like guests at a wedding: those favoring the defendant cross to his side, those with the prosecution take the other. Kyle has few people: a second-grade teacher from his Christian school and a former neighbor are two of them. It's freezing in here. Hot, almost, outside, unseasonable in March in Bellingham, so I'm wearing sandals, and my feet are so cold I surreptitiously cradle my toes with my fingers. The courthouse outside this room isn't cold and there are no signs of air-conditioning here; the room just seems suspended in its own field of unnatural frigidity, like Dante's Hell. I half expect to see Lucifer at the heart of it in his block of ice.

When I come in, a handful of women are sitting in the front row on the right, the prosecution side, talking about shampoo.

"I use Neutrogena but I'd like Pantene," says one, "if I could afford it."

"Take back your thirty cents, from yesterday," says somebody else.

"It's just thirty cents."

They seem like trial fans, T-shirted and chewing gum, joshing with the bailiffs, but they turn out to be the family of the victim, Thomas or Tommy Munsen. His young mother, Nora, and father, Thomas Sr., sit on the end. His mother has a rain of hair—straight, dark, and unnaturally perfect, like shiny and well-ironed fabric. She, too, tends toward T-shirts, gum, and teasing the bailiffs, particularly one Native American bailiff she nicknames Bam Bam. She's quieter than the others, and has been famously stoic throughout this ordeal; she will rarely cry at this trial.

Up front, behind the low wall separating us from the judge, jury, prosecution, and defendant and his team, a man arranges bags on a table; one clear one holds a large syringe.

"Giraffes today?" one of the Munsens asks him. He's Mac Setter, the prosecutor, who's brusque and businesslike and, improbably, wears an animal tie every day. The Munsens' shirts have things like Tweety Bird on them. Looked at this way the place has the feeling of an extraordinarily sober preschool.

One of my questions for myself, maybe part of my reason to return day after day, is whether if I were the dead boy's mother I would or could kill Kyle Anderson. When Tommy turned up dead, mutilated, I felt that I would—I'd have to—and Bruce and I ended up arguing the point a lot, me pro, him against.

This would come up, say, when we watched the news.

"I know what I'd do," I'd tell him. "Get a gun, shoot him during the perp walk."

"What good would that do?" Bruce has no idea, a better man than I am, as they say.

"It would just be what I'd have to do. I couldn't know he was out there." Secretly, in this fantasy, I plan to kill myself right afterward. This hypothetical death of a son does not seem to me a survivable event. Of course, I could just kill myself and let society enact its outrage on Kyle. But I know somehow this wouldn't be enough. I would have to shoot him, watch him bleed in front of me, though I don't believe in killing or vengeance. My body would make this decision. It would sense the vastness of this loss, deep within itself—a place that would now be ragged and empty—and in the universe.

So this would be the cure: to watch Kyle bleed in front of me. A void for a void. It would be, perhaps, a living metaphor.

When my target arrives, he looks not just young—eighteen is young, and he's a young eighteen—but extraordinarily harmless. Kyle Anderson turns out to be a fleshy boy, not fat but doughy, with a crew cut of white-blond hair, a strongly upturned nose, and an equally recessive chin. He looks different from my vague neighborhood memories of him: this is not the face I'm here for. He looks Woody Woodpeckerish—more likely to be a victim than a killer. He walks into the courtroom between two bailiffs, with his eyes straight ahead and a lack of expression that appears willed. As soon as Kyle appears, the man on the end of the first Munsen row, Tommy Munsen's grandfather, puts his head down and begins to sob, helplessly. Tommy's father Thomas pats him awkwardly on the back.

A LARGE PART of what I do in the courtroom, which has its share of downtime, is revisit this question of killing the boy, which morphs when I have to look for seven hours a day at the actual doughy neck and whitish tufty hair of this young killer. The back of his neck, vulnerable as the neck of any boy, has a lumpiness to it; could I do violence to this? I'm awed at first by how easy it would be. Our courthouse, which I haven't set foot in since finalizing Jin's adoption, has no security system, though metal detectors and security guards at courthouses have become routine. Here I wander in and a young female receptionist offers some kind of a nod without looking up from her desk. I shift uncomfortably from foot to foot, expecting her to ask me probing questions. She never looks up. I could be carrying an Uzi, waiting for the Kyle Andersons of the world to shuffle past so I can pick them off.

I'm startled again when Kyle comes into the courtroom, maybe primed by too much bad TV to have orange jumpsuits and foot chains in the back of my mind. Two large bailiffs escort him but he could bolt or grab someone or throw himself at the evidence if he really wanted to. The bailiffs lead Kyle to his table, where he'll sit, day after day, flanked by his two lawyers, the older man who does most of the talking and the young woman who seems to be the only person in the courtroom he has any real affinity with—he smiles at her, even teases her once. He wears, day after day, a pale blue shirt with a cream-colored cable-knit sweater.

So he brushes past me, within inches, and I could reach out and do anything to him I wanted to do. And he brushes past Nora Munsen just as close, several times a day, his molecules infecting the air she breathes, his body making a slight breeze, within reach of her hands.

The next day I'll see the victim's mother, in her veil of hair, wash her hands in the women's restroom next to a defense attorney, a woman contesting Kyle's guilt, at an adjoining sink.

THE MICE STORY ends this way. We begin with humane traps, and predictably lame results. The little smears of peanut butter in the traps can't compete with what crumbs we unthinkingly drop. Not a single mouse gets relocated, though we've promised them a drive to a beautiful woodland south of town. They stay and proliferate; I catch them running through the kitchen; they gnaw parts of my wood pantry into a fluff of nesting material.

Worse than anything is the scrabbling in the walls. I can't stand it at night when I'm trying to sleep, from behind us, and above us in the crawl space. *Scritch, scritch,* urgently soft. It feels, though we know it isn't, like something restless, desperately trapped.

I become more and more terrified of that sound, and in what's no doubt some weird displacement, I develop a phobia that we're all going to get hantavirus—a fatal disease carried by mice, but deer mice, not house mice like our cartoonish creatures. Phobias live their own lives, however, and mine becomes overwhelming, possessing me when I'm at home. I can't go into the basement at all because of the mouse scat there, so I can't do laundry or fetch a jar of my jam. When I see the mice upstairs, or hear them, or notice their leavings, I sob. I'm Lysoling everything, the air we breathe. Bruce keeps trying to reason with me, which makes things worse; personally, I don't mind, but my phobia gets furious about it. I'm not someone anyone can live with right now. We begin to modify our sanctity-of-life stance and try poison, which also does nothing. Finally we get an exterminator, who fills our house with pretty much the same poison, but at least the karma's on his head.

Bruce, as instructed by the exterminator, fills up the cracks in our basement walls—which the mice seem to be using as a way in—with some weird orange Martian ooze. It takes months of all this, but eventually the mice seem to die.

ONE OF THE UNDISPUTED FACTS of this case is that Tommy Munsen died of a massive overdose of insulin, some 100 times a therapeutic dose. Kyle adapted tubing and a giant syringe to create an instrument that could deliver that much of the drug. He did other, extremely violent things to the boy, any one of which could have killed Tommy, but the coroner's guess is that the insulin was the cause of death, and Kyle's fascination with toxic substances will come up again and again.

Kyle had syringes in his room; he'd been stealing them from his school first-aid cabinet and possibly from a diabetic family friend. He had vials of poisons, insulin, another toxin called myristicin, a concentrated form of a chemical that occurs naturally in nutmeg and parsley.

An FBI witness, Madeline Montgomery, a poison expert who's crisp, attractive, straight out of Central Casting, reconstructs this teenager's room, full of secreted poisons and poison delivery systems.

As testimony progresses, members of the Munsen group rise periodically to spit out their gum. Grandparents, aunts, uncles, cousins, a friend or two: people affiliated with the family come and go, so the number varies, usually a dozen or so, and at first I'm aware of them more for their gum than any display of feeling. The bailiffs, two slow and enormous men, chew gum all day too, but it's a slow chew, a pass-the-time chew, a small and chronic motion of the jaw, a chaw that seems to match the steady process of the day and thereby the planet and thereby the world. The Munsens chew as if masticating the event.

Thomas Munsen Sr. sits hunched forward, a roundedness in the front row. He's brown-haired like his wife, though Tommy had that light blond crew cut, an upturned nose: in fact, a passing resemblance to the Andersons.

The bailiffs never seem to spit out their gum, while the Munsens toss theirs all the time.

Perhaps, I think, killing Kyle would be easy.

The things in the world waiting to harm our children are innumerable. We all know that. Jin, fiddling around with a small toy, says to me one day, "If you live, you die. If you die, you live."

"That's awfully philosophical," I tell him.

"Why?"

"Isn't it?"

"No. It's just this game I'm playing."

He is playing some kind of a game, with a small ball. I'm about to tell him how this comment fits with many concepts of the soul, but decide this is not what's called for. He may have his own concept of the soul, or just inadvertently be talking like a Desert Father. Kids do that, in between blasting you with squirt guns and discussing poo. Either way, I don't really care: lately I've been feeling that I intrude myself philosophically into his heart and mind too much, as parents do, trying to leave bits of themselves there.

I want to let him determine how to take his living and dying. Maybe I'm just too preoccupied with the bald-faced facts of those things. I want him safe. No mice in the house, no cars going way too fast on my street, no Kyle Andersons.

Jin at six can be mouthy and disobedient; he unlatches the front gate and runs down the street, though the rule is he stays in the yard. He bolts across the street without permission. I create consequences, restrict him to the backyard. When I get so angry I start to lose my temper I stop and smell him, the clean child smell. Sooner or later he has to be allowed to try again, and sooner or later temptation becomes too much. It's all part of growing up, I tell myself, and other parents tell me. And every year, every day, a certain number of children have to be sacrificed to the gods of growing up.

(*I hate to think,* said a neighbor, *Tommy died to save all our little boys.*)

If any child can be saved by watching, by a love that feels as physically real as asbestos, by sheer will alone, it will be mine, I tell myself. And in this thought I betray the still, stoic woman in her rain of hair.

. . .

I WILL TELL YOU, later, that Kyle Anderson had been waiting for a boy. Now I'll relate how Tommy Munsen came to be the boy. Tommy had been riding his bicycle around the block when he stopped at the Anderson home, catty-corner to his own, looking for Kyle's brother Eric. He found Kyle, on a juvenile version of house arrest (for theft of a Palm Pilot), home alone working on a fishpond filter. Kyle loved to take things apart and to build fishponds, and Tommy hung around asking him questions about the pond. Tommy's persistence and questions somehow enraged Kyle—it was "the most ticked off he'd ever gotten," he said in his videotaped confession—and Kyle went and got a backpack containing duct tape, electrical tape, a razor, a dowel, insulin, the modified hypodermic needle, and a towel (all of which were ready, perhaps packed, for something that would come), and led Tommy down to a nearby brushy field, promising him a game.

After committing the murder, Kyle went back to his house, where an automated calling system monitored his house arrest; since he'd been discovered missing, he called his juvenile officer and said he'd gone for a walk because a neighbor kid wouldn't leave him alone. When Tommy's parents went to look for their son, Kyle came out and volunteered to help.

The next morning a woman walking a dog found Tommy's body. Based on the things done to the body, the killer seemed likely to be an adult, but Kyle got connected with the crime by a few things: Tommy's bike in front of his house; a neighbor who saw them together; and the violation of his house arrest. Under police questioning, Kyle kept making missteps in telling his story—mostly, detectives said, he was overdetailed, his story was too clear, too cogent—and finally he confessed. At the time he was sixteen.

KYLE ANDERSON, the now-eighteen-year-old whose curd-pale, lumpy, frail neck I look at day after day, has been a figure of enormous terror to my son. A boogeyman. When Jin couldn't sleep at night, this young man lurked in the closet, and Jin dreamed of the giant scissors that would cut Kyle out of jail, the weak walls that would fall out of his way. His nightmares have been driven by the two white hands I also see, projecting from the ends of the cream-colored cable-knit sleeves. I imagine Jin will dream these dreams in some way forever, as will I. Kyle is the X factor in my parenting, the boy who looks like a computer geek and lives a few doors away, with a head topped with a soft brush of platinum, a chin receding back of his lower lip, and a backpack with insulin, razor, tape, and towel.

And so I come back trying to make sense of him—perhaps at the end more than I need to destroy him—though this desire as I listen to testimony day after day becomes more and more frustrated. I realize that in the last two years I've been so swayed by how fiercely everyone around me's trying to explain the question posed by Kyle Anderson that I expect a witness to come in one day telling us for sure how Kyle could have incubated such a dream. Almost a little lecture: a pointer and a chart of his genome, or a slide show of his early childhood. And that will be that; I'll never have to return, freezing my tailbone on the defense's side because that's where all the empty spaces are.

"Bad genes," says the guy down the street, and that is that.

"Abused," say other friends. "I *know* it. A friend of a neighbor . . ."

"If you could just look into his brain," says Brooke, a psychiatric nurse-practitioner I see, "I'm convinced you would find something different. Terribly different."

In the middle of the trial I go crying to my priest and he says cryptically, "There are fallen angels out there," and quotes an old church father who wrote you would know the end times "when children are so evil even the demons are afraid."

All of this adds up to something that sits, specterlike and unholy, slightly to the right of this boy in the defendant's chair.

I FIND MYSELF admiring the defense attorney, Jon Ostlund, which surprises me, since I'm rooting—if you can call it that—so hard for the prosecution. He's an older man, pale and kindly. A woman named Lisa Waldvogel sits second chair. The defense has gone into this trial with the admission behind them that Kyle committed the crime. Even if they could somehow bar Kyle's confession, Ostlund's overwhelmed by physical evidence. Another FBI expert testifies to finding Tommy's blood on Kyle's shoes, on a towel in his backpack (during this witness, Baechtel's, testimony, Kyle inexplicably starts giggling at his female attorney). Several dog walkers saw Kyle at the scene.

What we'll decide here in the courtroom is Kyle's intent. Essentially, he stands trial for what lay in his head that day, for the level of consciousness of his choice. The judgment will be first-degree or second-degree murder; first-degree kidnapping; or the lesser charge of unlawful imprisonment. No one can even argue whether Kyle had intent to kill. He did. But in this moment we freeze and hold up for examination, do his acts show premeditation, or impulse? How can we ink this thought and trace it to its final resting place?

Ostlund, who's pale in a sweet way, not the sunless way Kyle is, asks a Detective Green what Kyle told him about the crime.

"He said it was 'the most ticked off' he'd ever gotten," says Green. "He said he was not in his 'right mind.'"

The prosecutor counters this by having Green go through the lies in Anderson's videotaped testimony: that he found the razor and other implements he used in the grass rather than bringing them from his bedroom, other statements to indicate he had not packed a backpack, including a towel, to bring with him to that field.

TRIALS HAVE this compelling air of minutiae: a series of questions goes to whether Kyle could or couldn't read *Harry Potter*. I find myself writing, *Point of these questions?* a lot in my notebook. Who cares if he could read *Harry Potter*? Apparently Kyle's fundamentalist mother found the book demonic. I don't think anyone would argue that drove him to kill. Jerri Anderson, Kyle's mother, sometimes took her son off his medication, thinking God would heal him; I see the relevance of this, but no one argues his impulses changed either way. I want to get up and start insisting on my own questions, what they all think about that cloud of evil—if it's a product of a mind apart, or if evil lives its own life, and occasionally touches down somewhere.

And even if it's the latter, are some of us more susceptible than others to its touchdowns? I think of myself at ten, writing that journal entry: *I think I'm possessed by the devil.* No explanation. What did I feel at the time? What, perhaps, had I done?

As if to seal us to these questions of the mind, this room concedes nothing to the body: so overwhelmingly wooden—the walls, the hard pews, and the clock over the black-robed judge's shoulder. The Munsen family brings their own cushions to sit on, boxes of tissue, and water, in addition to their gum.

And so the psychiatric witnesses seem like oracles. Reporters show up for them. Except for the closing and the sentencing, both of which are packed with journalists down from Vancouver and up from Seattle, most trial days two reporters come, one from the local paper and one from the local radio station, and sit in for an hour or two. They like testimony from family members and psychiatrists and don't come for forensics. Both reporters—women—are striking, svelte and well dressed, with dark hair, in the mode of Madeline Montgomery, the poison expert: crisp as communion wafers. Dark-haired women are a countertheme in this trial involving tragic blond boys.

The reporters sit together making small talk, applying Chap-Stick, and exchanging mints called Myntz.

"You look good in pink."

"Thanks."

I ask the *Herald* reporter one day if this kind of story doesn't bother her. She gives me that classic American answer, "It's just my job," and a shrug. She's really quite pretty, in a dark, Spanish sort of way, and young; she could model. "Maybe it would be different if I had kids."

The two therapists are defense witnesses. Before they testify, the jury's excused and the lawyers argue whether to present evidence on the mental condition of Kyle's younger brother and his mother. The defense wants it in. Ostlund wants to bring in Kyle's home environment, but the testimony's finally excluded. The first psychiatrist, who saw Kyle several years before the murder, diagnosed him with ADHD and depression, calling him "distractible, somewhat hyperactive, but often passive and quiet, impulsive." His testimony consists largely of Ostlund reinforcing his, Dr. Starn's, belief that kids with ADHD lack any impulse control.

Here's a part of Mac Setter's cross:

"How many kids have you treated with ADHD?" (Answer: Hundreds.) "How many of them have killed?"

The defense objects before Starn answers.

The other psychiatric witness saw Kyle eight times, up to a few days before the murder. He's a psychologist, Nicholas Pahl, a man with an oddly absent and diffident way of talking; he keeps referring to Mike and Jerri Anderson as "Dad" and "Mom," as if we're all part of this weird extended family.

"Dad was gone a lot," he says of Mike, who drove a soft drink truck. "There were a lot of issues with Mom, rage at Mom." Kyle sits through this testimony, reading his lawyers' notes. His cartoonish face, with its puffy cheeks and nose canted upward, stays impassive. Nora Munsen, who left during part of the earlier arguments, returns, back straight, hair even more perfect than usual. Pahl, too, diagnosed ADHD, plus a learning disorder, and possible kleptomania. The boy had taken to stealing things, and occasionally setting fires. Pahl made a note to rule out schizoid personality disorder in the future. ("Kyle was too young at sixteen for such a diagnosis," he said.) He listed schizoid personality disorder symptoms: pattern of detachment, flattened emotions, taking pleasure in few activities, coldness, little or no normal developmental sexual interest.

At the last point, Nora Munsen slumps over, like a column toppling, and cries on her husband's back.

"Kyle looks at people as objects," says Pahl. Nora Munsen gets up and leaves again.

Like Starn, Pahl faces sharp cross-examination by Setter, who has Pahl read off some of his own clinical notes, listing Kyle as "low risk."

"I thought Kyle had a serious mental and psychiatric disorder," Pahl says stiffly. "I had no idea how he was going to conduct himself in the future. So far he had had an ability to conduct himself with other people."

Pahl's not a strong witness, coming across as a mix of bureaucratic and hapless, and Setter barks questions at him, many of which seem designed to get information out. He has Pahl recite details of the crime. Kyle collected syringes and knives as well as pictures of young children in varying stages of undress that he ripped out of magazines; he arranged the photos on a tray along with razors and syringes. (I come to think of this as the "death tray.") Fascinated with Nazi war criminals and their human experiments, he collected articles with titles like "Killing with Syringes."

No one blinks or sighs or dips a head. We listen to this testimony without emotion. I wonder if, in this room, we've all come down with schizoid personality disorder.

MY OWN MOROSE DR. L., with his wrinkled-olive face, could have sat in a witness chair testifying to my awful strangeness: or at least, I hear this as a chime behind this testimony.

"He really wouldn't talk to me," says Pahl. "There wasn't much I could do."

"She wouldn't talk to me," says L. "She was a lost girl when she came in."

At sixteen—a year after seeing L., the age of Kyle at the time of the murder—I had a serious drug problem, using psychedelics and, especially, narcotics every day. Doctors later charitably called it my "self-medicating phase." However you justify this time, it formed a part of my life when an on-again, off-again boyfriend named Kevin cut another man named John-John's hand off, a fact I recorded in my journal, at the end of a long entry on trying to buy marijuana, with a careless *I wasn't scared or anything, just fascinated. Also, I felt really badly for John-John. Shit, he has enough problems.*

THE JUDGE, confronting Kyle at the sentencing, will say, "I don't know what went wrong. Maybe nobody held you when you were a baby. But nothing I say can give you empathy."

Is this how you get empathy? I want to ask. Is this what's wrong? I think back to my childhood, the Baby Boom era of the fifties and early sixties, the time of the cocktail hour, babies made with the aim of their being seen and not heard. My parents' sense of parenting had been borrowed from the hardscrabble soil of other parts of the world, where you measured your success by feeding children well, getting them to grow higher than you had grown—like a crop of corn loved because you have made the earth do the barely possible: stay healthy.

"You get good food in your belly." My father once erupted with this statement at dinner. It had very little context, as I remember. He sat at his place at the head of the table, with one child of his at each side, and a regular dinner, probably something like spaghetti or meatloaf. This was simply a statement of his triumph.

I remember, vaguely, my parents after consulting with Dr. L., when he said, with me somewhere in the room, that they could only expect a lifetime of institutions for this hopelessly schizophrenic girl. I don't remember him listing symptoms or a rationale, or if he knew the degree of my drug use, though maybe he did all those things. My mother and father saddened, collapsed a little in the cheek, but did not disbelieve him.

SO I HAVE COME to this courtroom to psychically kill this boy, but soon I have to face the question of how I am not him. I may remember the story of Dr. L. almost as a dream, but not the way he looked at me, at this face of mine that held nothing he wanted to hear: his small eyes shrunk in the pupil with a contempt that came from deep within, from the brain stem of this man who'd looked at too many wholly poor specimens of humanity.

My friends would tell you—and I would too, I guess—that I have empathy, the normal amount at least, maybe more. My empathy extends from mice to humans. And there's a difference between manic depression and schizoid personality disorder, based on the testimony I'm hearing: the former so overwhelmingly emotional, porous.

Still, when Pahl testifies about Kyle's lack of sense of himself—he picked his nose constantly, rarely bathed—I can't help but look down at my half-shaved legs, my overgrown toenails, and bra straps that stick out, things I don't notice until the svelte female reporters turn away from me with just enough dismissiveness to show they place me nowhere in their planetary orbit. My students, for whom I have all empathy, catch me wearing clothes inside out.

"The hardest thing in the world to understand," my brother Chris once said, "is that other people are just as real as you are." Most people never do, I said, or maybe he did. Obviously that girl who wrote about severed limbs with a Taliban-like obliviousness had some problems with this. Not that I harmed anything; rather, I picked up stray cats and dropped chicks like some kind of drug-fueled impound service. This had been my habit since the time my family moved from that apartment in Elizabeth, New Jersey, into a small house, when I was seven. Though my father, who doesn't love animals, didn't allow me to bring creatures home, I hid them in the basement. I was a stubborn child, hyperfocused. I brought home cats who caught mice, and if the mice were hurt and not dead I kept them, too, in cages—tooth wounds like pencil stabs—until they healed. Several wild mice bit me.

Once at twelve I found an infant squirrel that had somehow gotten out of the nest; you could see its heart through the tissue-thin latex of its pink skin. I found a book somewhere that explained how to feed a baby squirrel warm milk through an eye-dropper every two hours, warning that it would probably die any-way. I named my squirrel Socrates and decided it would survive, through the power of my will. It died anyway. I went into a ter-rible storm of grieving, hours of thrown-on-the-bed sobs, the kind of display a spurned media keeps itching to get from Nora Munsen. My father yelled that there'd be no more animals in our house, in a fit of irritation, and something more than irritation.

I ignored him. And I give this all as testimony to my empathy, which I want to believe in: but I have that hand lost in my diary, immobile, accusing. Even Hitler had his Blondi, his German shep-herd that he loved. Did I have a time when I could have been—neuroatypical as I was, my mind pushed around by itself and by what I fed into it—something like this boy of the sad, unlovable neck, not in his actions but in some deadness inside?

Or perhaps I should worry now, mice-killing healed woman.

BY DAY FIVE the courtroom has become a strange place. Some-body on my campus has offered extra credit for attending the trial, and students have begun wandering in throughout the day, rifling through their backpacks for a handout called "Specific writ-ing assignment criteria," fumbling for pens and scribbling what-ever drama or trivia happens to be coming from the front of the room. Some stay ten minutes, then leave, regardless of the testi-mony, scrawling notes fast to grab their credit. Some pull out books to read and try to nibble quietly on granola bars, though of course that's impossible in such a small room, and we all stare at their crinkling and crunching. They whisper loud questions to one another, asking who's on trial, what for.

In any case, two-thirds of the way through the trial, the courtroom's composed of a portion of people who care passionately about the outcome (the Munsens), a portion who seem barely aware that they're not in a dorm room, and the motley crew of others (me, the reporters who observe for an hour or two a day, the former neighbor and the teacher of Kyle), who are in some other place entirely. The latter two women seem to be there in some kind of solidarity with the Anderson family, though when Kyle looks around the courtroom he doesn't acknowledge them.

After Nicholas Pahl, Kyle's father Mike gets recalled to the stand. He's absolutely stolid, with his head marble-erect on a spine that seems calcified, a columnar twin to Nora Munsen. His face, though, mirrors his son's astonishingly, with the same nose, chin, hair, and pallor; when he takes the stand, I see who Kyle will become in jail.

Kyle does not react to his father. So far, his humanness emerges only for the young, female second-chair defense attorney, another woman with long dark hair, albeit one who looks slightly less at home in her chunky heels and tailored suits than the reporters. Kyle smiles at her sometimes, makes eye contact, teases her one day when she spills water.

Ostlund has Mike Anderson read underlining in an industrial first aid book the family owned, testify the underlines are his, not Kyle's. Routine stuff.

Mac Setter gets up to do his cross.

"Does your son have empathy?"

Mike Anderson's stoic face struggles, just a little; he hesitates; the muscles of his cheeks swim and think. He has no idea what answer is called for here.

"Well," he says finally, "he loves his grandfather."

SOMETHING ELSE IMPROBABLE has happened by day five. I've started feeling sorry for Kyle. At some moments the feeling's quite gut-level and overwhelming, though it intersects not at all with my sense of the necessity of killing him. There's never anyone on his side of the courtroom, except those of us just looking for a seat—and even random visitors gravitate to the prosecution side, where the view of the screen's better—and the former teacher and neighbor, who seem empathic with Kyle but not exactly supporting. His mother doesn't attend. I'm told by the reporter she came once. After Mike Anderson testifies, he sits in on the trial, accompanied twice by an older man who looks to be Kyle's grandfather; Kyle beams at him, reminding me of Mike's comment that his grandfather is the man he loves.

So Kyle's side of the courtroom by the end of the trial has the motley crew and two family members, both upright in the same stiff position with their arms crossed. Neither man touches Kyle, though they could. He's only a few feet away, and his shoulder looks concave and tender; you can see a hand settling on it, you want that, though this body's done something so cruel. They could clasp him, even, when he walks in and out. I settle into being this parent for a while, with Jin having done something monstrous. I still carry him on my hip sometimes, though he's improbably long as a hip child, legs dangling nearly to the floor. I would hold him no matter what he did, maybe even grasp him tighter, trying to pull him back into the private world of my family from the public one of law. Not that I think any deprivation of Kyle's flesh explains him; I don't. All I can tell you is that three-quarters of the way through the trial I feel in a place deep within my abdomen the abandonment of Kyle's body as well as the rip of Tommy's violation.

As you can imagine, this feeling poses problems for my assassination fantasies, though as I said they don't go away, or even become less intense. What does happen is that I begin to look at Kyle's exposed neck as if it—in some isolated way—is a victim of violence; I see my own feelings cutting into him like a razor, into his uncaressed nakedness. Mentally I lift my hand and I can't do it.

So I settle on the idea of poison. Throughout the day the prosecution and defense pour themselves glass after glass of water. When images appear on the screen and people crowd around the front of the room, against the wooden ledge separating spectators from the court, it seems easy to slip something into Kyle's cup. Or hand him a laced Coke, a peaceful poison like the hemlock the Greeks favored, or one of Kyle's own serums that I've never heard of, stopping his heart.

THE LAST DAY of the trial, the day of closing arguments, is a circus. News crews come in from the cities and, of course, they have no clue who anybody is.

"Do you know what they look like?" a Canadian reporter says to his cameraman on the steps of the courthouse, about who knows who. Students whisper, "It's him!" when they see Kyle. Reporters press business cards on various members of the Munsen family, and on Mike Anderson, asking for comments, anytime; the families say "No comment, no comment" blankly, like children rehearsing the alphabet. Jon Ostlund greets his client with an ostentatious "Good morning, Kyle!" when he walks into the courtroom. Nora Munsen wears a black Looney Tunes shirt; Mac Setter wears a hippo tie. There's some semiotics of clothing here, something I can't fathom. Every day Kyle Anderson wears the same pale blue shirt and cream sweater; Ostlund and Setter always wear the same-color suits, with Setter's minute tie menagerie setting him apart.

"WE HAVE EXHIBIT NUMBER 149, a folding knife. Several razor knives, two more folding knives, a piece of a pool cue recovered from Kyle's closet, a piece of a broom handle with duct tape, lengths of dowel, an arrow . . ."

Two strange things here: one is that I can't follow the number of weapons in Kyle's room, this boy who lived four blocks from me. The other is that all this information is being introduced into evidence by the defense. Ostlund, who has been a careful and thoughtful attorney in a tough case, opens the defense with a move that seems remarkably self-defeating.

"Two more razor knives, more dowel . . ." "Killing with Syringes," a Nazi article, based on experiments at Auschwitz.

WHEN I WAS A WILD GIRL OF FIFTEEN, hopeless, I had a boyfriend who slept—I slept with him—with a weapon of some sort tacked up over the bed. I think it was a gun; he had guns, anyway, but it may have been a knife, and whatever it was, he doted on it. This boyfriend owned a number of guns; most of the boys I knew did; they were drug dealers. It seems strange to me now that I didn't learn to shoot at that point in my life, but I did only later, when some Georgia landlords amused themselves teaching the Yankee girl to plug Coke cans with a rifle, something I turned out, with my keen eyesight, to be remarkably good at. Kyle, who's been distant from every human who's testified, even his father, looks up avidly as his weapons get displayed, as if he expects us all to be impressed.

Ostlund's strategy is to argue that the relatively meager weapons Kyle took to the field—hypodermic, insulin, razor, dowel—don't show much premeditation, just a chance to do a little of the experimentation he'd become so fascinated by. Ostlund doesn't disagree that Kyle, with his death tray stacked with surgical neatness—the lined-up knives and taped photos cut out from magazines, children clean in their uncomplicated bodies—planned to kill a little boy; just not this one, this time. Not *planned* quite.

"Intent," he says, "is not premeditation."

At another point today he says, in a statement that may be as empty or as profound as words get, "Kyle is who Kyle is."

Ostlund argues that Kyle didn't know how much insulin would kill the child: that with his almost sexual attraction to injections (he also collected photos of people receiving shots), he only planned to give him the hypodermic. Kyle killed Tommy more or less by accident, Ostlund says, and only then decided to use his body for "medical experimentation." Ostlund cites Kyle's "interest in the mechanics of things."

It sounds as though maybe I should be disgusted by Ostlund now, invested as I am in Kyle's conviction of the maximum charges. But no, not at all; he's just doing his job, in that most American of ways of bumbling through the moral quagmire that is this world. And he and the woman attorney feel like the closest Kyle has to family, and for that I must bless them a little; they pour him water, ask him how he's doing once in a while, smile, acknowledge the child in him while the law adjudicates the adult.

Who knows what Ostlund could have done with this case if he'd been able to use evidence about Kyle's mother—what tears might have come on the other side of the room—or perhaps that amounted to nothing at all. In any case, he doesn't have much, and he does what he can with what he has.

It's Setter, a clenched fist of an attorney with that improbable light detail of the animal ties, who gets the cameras rolling. He has the coroner's testimony to work with, the story of Tommy's death. Taped up, choked manually and with a dowel. Lethal injection of some 100 times the normal dose of insulin, amputation of ear, nose, nipple, and genitals, the last amputated in pieces, one testicle never found. No face left, with his ear sliced off and nose cut apart—it appeared Kyle lifted up the nose to look into Tommy's head—and the duct-taped mouth and his throat slit open just short of decapitation. A double-Y autopsy, one large Y covering the torso and a smaller inverted one in the pelvic area. Back slit open along the backbone, rectum cut. Bruised bone from the knife's intense pressure. Most cutting postmortem, some pre-. Some perimortem, meaning whether before or after death can't be judged.

This information floats past my head into the air. It is, literally, beyond me. Just a few things land: like that Kyle would have gotten close enough to smell that boy. The mutilation of something fresher than innocence. My insides tear for the parents, for whom all this has to become real.

The coroner estimates this work on the body would have taken an hour or more. At first police believed the killer was a medical student or veterinarian or even a mortician; the cutting had professionalism as well as viciousness.

ODDLY ENOUGH, or perhaps not, since my town becomes a small town after a while, one of the people first on the crime scene turned out to be a member of my congregation, Troy. Later he drove a wooden cross into the ground.

"He heard a horrible scream coming out of nowhere, there was no one there," my priest Father Joseph tells me later, "and he was freaked out and called me." Father Joseph came and blessed not only the field that had held Tommy's body but all of my neighborhood, my street, my neighbors' streets and houses and the yards where my son plays, or spats, with his friends.

"There was a cloud of evil there that day," he tells me. And he doesn't mean evil as played in the movies, by striking Irish actor Gabriel Byrne.

My priest has a look somewhere between a raffish older movie actor like Albert Finney and Father Christmas: white hair, florid, eyes both shivery blue and warm. He's handsome, and loves slivovitz. He works at a hospice and encounters the unearthly a lot, like near-death experiences, coming across them the way we encounter those phone solicitors who try but don't quite connect, the clicking on the line, mysterious and routine.

YOU WANT TO DISBELIEVE HIM, and I do, too. But I have my own story that you won't believe, though if you came into my yard I could show you at least a fragment of it. The week after the trial it hailed Stendhal. Or, at least, I learned then it had hailed Stendhal in the winter. Sometime during those weeks I noticed books, old-looking, flung around on my neighbor Dean's roof, open. I assumed his boys had tossed them up there somehow, but when I saw Dean walking around on his roof that week I asked him about it and he told me in his matter-of-fact way that they fell down from the sky.

"Want one?" he said, and threw me a book, Stendhal's diary, and the frontispiece of another one. The books were at least a hundred years old and pulling apart, half mold now.

Dean, a locksmith and inventor of mechanical things like a solar-powered three-wheel bike, said during a snowstorm books fell up and down our alley; after he told me that I started noticing pages, bindings stuck here and there, like between our fence and the next one.

"Maybe they fell out of a plane or something," he said. He just wanted them off his roof.

THE NIGHT of the sentencing I ran into the bathroom suddenly and threw up and threw up and threw up.

My friends—and, I suppose, nonfriends, too—kept asking me

why I went to this trial. Why do this to yourself? they said, and I got angry, thinking the crime had been done in a certain way to me: not that I had the grief of the victim's family, but I had my son's nightmares, my terror of letting him out of my sight. My sense of the vulnerability of his body. Only limited details of the crime were released, but when they were released, he became to me a tissue of tender openings. His sense of that vulnerability, my fearless one.

But I ended up saying, "Well, it happened so close to me and, you know, I'm a writer." Doing my job, in other words.

Of course, I don't know why I did this to myself either. I know I felt overwhelmed by what brushed against my life and could have destroyed it. I wanted to see Kyle put away. Maybe more, I wanted someone to explain Kyle to me and separate him from me. And it always seemed like we were just one witness away from that, though the clues to his psyche only became more and more wildly conflicting. It became as mindless as putting coins in a slot machine, waiting for the icons that never quite line up.

WHAT WE HAD, with my neighbor Kyle's tucked chin, cartoonish face: a boy who collected enough weapons to power a desert army and rare poisons, who taught himself as a teenager how to do a particular type of autopsy peculiar to the East Coast, studied Nazi killing, all with the intent to kill a child. My child as easily as anyone's, I imagine, half a mile from his house.

What we had to explain him: ADHD; possibly poor parenting; possibly too little touch; possibly a personality disorder that no doubt hundreds of thousands of people have; evil.

. . .

I HAVE TWO THEORIES weighing on me, and I have been torn between them so I'll tell you both.

There is in my questioners' voices sometimes a trill not of *Why this horror?* but simply of *Why think about this?* The killer lived four blocks from me and I saw him and his victim around, in that careless not-seeing way you reserve for your own places. I strolled my child asleep past the house where Kyle lived, with American flags and a swing set. As my son grew into his long and lithe body, those dissecting eyes of Kyle's must have seen him many times, and maybe it doesn't add up to anything, maybe it's just the world we live in now.

Theory two: that Kyle stands as a koan or theological knot unto himself, but he's like one of those theologies that tell you that trying to understand the nature of the Trinity is like trying to carry the ocean with a small bucket, so I can't go any farther than this; as Augustine said of evil, "Do not seek to know more than is appropriate."

TWO WEEKS after the trial's close, hollow, unable to write, I decide one day to consult Stendhal. Because of his bad odor and habit of shredding off in our hands, he's been consigned to a dilapidated outbuilding we call the dog cottage. I've known people in my life who've randomly opened Bibles to answer their questions, and given the biblical way this book came into my life ("a plague of Stendhals," we've come to call that night of hailing books), I'm treating it the same way.

"Since my last entry I have killed three hares, the first quadrupeds of my life," Stendhal tells me, when I flop the diary open.

IT'S THE END OF MARCH, a few weeks from the second anniversary of the murder, and once again we're in the courtroom, crammed in this time, for the sentencing. Those out-of-town journalists are back, with reporters telling the camera people where to pan and who to stop on for reaction shots. The Munsen family moan, "Sit here. Don't let the reporters sit with us," when people they know come in. Students arrive, still with study guides and still apparently seeking credit. I'm surrounded by the clack of "No comment, no comment" from both sides of the aisle, a phrase that has become rote. The beautiful reporter Chap-Sticking, the judge in his black robes that seem to say in this place he's removed from the concerns of the body. Everyone doing a job.

The jury's already returned a verdict of guilty on the maximum counts, aggravated murder and aggravated kidnapping, so the drama's not so much the sentencing as the time when the victim's family speaks. The Munsens have chosen Wayne Smith, one of Tommy's grandfathers, as spokesman, though the comments were prepared on behalf of the family by an aunt. Before he reads the prepared statement, Smith says a few words himself, and all this attribution confuses the reporters; most of the papers get it wrong the next day.

For himself, Smith says, he does not think justice was done. Kyle should be put to death. The prosecution bargained away the death penalty a long time ago in this case; it's rarely applied to one so young.

"You are evil," Smith reads from the statement, flanked by Nora and Thomas Munsen Sr. and other family members. "You deserve a tortured existence."

Smith delivers his words in a monotone: "Why is it an innocent, unspeaking boy should suffer for your own dark fantasies"— and only here does the local reporter in front of me start writing. "We believe this trial was the crowning moment of your life," giving Kyle, he says, complete attention and control.

A reporter from Channel 7 in Seattle frantically directs her cameraman toward different reaction shots.

"There is no forgiveness in my heart," says Smith. "After today, you don't exist."

If you could see this statement, Smith adds at the end, speaking directly to Kyle, "you'd see that your name is in the lower-case. We no longer consider you a person."

Wayne Smith's a slight man who gives his statement in a monotone that emphasizes minor words—the *the*'s and *a*'s and *do*'s, the way an airline announcer would—and jumbles up the tragedy of the loss with the trivial, like its timing at the start of baseball season. As I listen to him I betray the Munsen family again. As a writer I think of how much better I would do. Nobody in this courtroom would be dry-eyed, I think. As soon as this thought crosses my mind, I hate myself.

Kyle, the boy-turned-man and the man now doomed to personlessness, sits unmoved, even as the judge lashes out at him for his deadpan attitude through the trial. Hard to tell what this attitude means, as Kyle sits surrounded by cameras—one has been allowed into the judge and jury's area—with booms hanging down for sound, and I wonder if he'd behave differently without them. As it is, it feels like it's become his job to remain deadpan and absorb the verdict of evil, pure and unredeemable, we're gathered to heap upon him. Which isn't to say he hasn't earned that verdict; Satan himself, no doubt, would play to the cameras.

And what, I wonder, would I do? Though I'm not him. I haven't poured a child's face into the ground.

Of course I remember once sitting helpless and confused as someone declared me unfit to live inside the largish bounds of culture.

Scritch, scritch in the walls.

When the sentence comes down, Mike's stalwart neighbor, Mia, lays a hand on his shoulder. "Sorry, Mike," she says softly, not for any reporters to hear. He shrugs, a gesture eloquent in its absence of any eloquence. His pale face, the Dorian Gray image of his son's, remains the same.

JUST YESTERDAY, writing, I heard a young mother shooing her children across campus; they weren't going fast enough for her and she hissed, *Ten strokes of the belt when we get home*, and when I looked I saw only the little boy, from the back, black hair and that little boy neck, with the ears and the whiteness between the ears like the fragile pages of a book.

Ten strokes for each of you, and his shoulders explained her seriousness.

Back at the trial Kyle sits there refracting our expectations of him. I hover over him two times, once as doppelgänger, the child who society decides has strayed irredeemably far from its practices of mind.

I also use the commotion to do what as a mother I know needs to be done, slipping drops into a Dixie cup of water. I have a handgun weighing down my purse, but looking at the back of that head I could never cause it to fracture, close-cropped, alternately smooth and bumped, dog-eared as it is.

Kyle gets sentenced to, as we like to say it, *life*.

I would look around the courtroom, fixing my eyes on his father and grandfather, willing them to get up. Willing someone to touch him, maybe just once and just on the shoulder, but with pressure and for some time. Then I would give him the cup.

I AM THE NAME IT HAD

We stand, in a manner of speaking, midway between the
unpredictability of atoms and the unpredictability of God.

—FREEMAN DYSON

Have you discovered the beginning, that you can ask
about the end?

—THE GNOSTIC GOSPEL OF THOMAS

AFTER THE TRIAL, around the time of Kyle Anderson's
sentencing, my church moves from our old building—the
Mole's funeral home, where we rented the chapel once a
week—to a karate academy, where we rent the floor space once
a week. The karate academy has been operating for years out of,
as it happens, an old church, so now we have a spire and a balcony
with pews, along with numchucks, swords, and a sparring dummy
who's usually swathed in a white sheet with a prop underneath
giving him outstretched arms: he's something holy and terrible
from the Old Testament. The academy's a crumbly building—the
loppy spire is, well, uninspiring—in a studenty part of town.
Sprung couches and plastic chairs on lawns and porches. At least
our new home has the accoutrements of a church, if we can ignore the numchucks and sparring dummys.

Not everyone at St. Nicholas loves the new martial atmosphere, but most of us are happy to be away from the funeral home. It had a small room off the chapel—kind of an alcove—where we stored things: the children often wandered there, playing hide-and-seek, and it held occupied coffins from time to time. Once, for some reason a coffin lid had been propped open. Somehow the open coffin—which had a woman in it—got us all to giggling. I mean, way too much. So:

"Oh, good," says Jin cheerfully, about the move to the karate church. "We won't have to worry about dead people anymore."

It never occurred to me we were worrying about dead people. As I talked it over with him, it seemed clear that Jin wasn't worrying about them, just feeling he didn't like the limits they imposed on hide-and-seek, even from their place on the other side of the cosmic order. We seem to be a group of people that has a great deal of truck—enough of it pleasant—with the dead. A very gentle, lovely, older woman who attends the church, named Barbara, lost her ninety-nine-year-old mother recently.

"I see her all the time," she said right after her mother Flossie's death. We're standing outside the doors to the karate church when she pops out with this, next to the flaking mural of a dragon painted on the side of the building, above the word *Karate*. Here we gather after the service to break our fast, those of us who hold to the practice of Sunday-morning fasting; we set out a folding table and chairs and eat cheese and muffins together. I think I must be choking on a saltine; I always thought Barbara pictured a lot of us as woo-woo, too willing to admit the touch of spirits.

"She came to the funeral," Barbara continues placidly, "but it bothered her. I saw her with her parents standing behind her and their parents behind them."

It is evident that God loves diversity. Perhaps the universe is constructed according to a principle of maximum diversity. The principle of maximum diversity says that the laws of nature, and the initial conditions at the beginning of time, are such as to make the universe as interesting as possible. As a result, life is possible but not too easy. Maximum diversity often leads to maximum stress.

These are the words of Princeton physicist Freeman Dyson. Things like life and consciousness will evolve to create diversity, though they do not have to, and in fact, consciousness will yield intelligence and all the joy and pain that go with it, as well as a sense of its own brief edges. Life could easily—very easily—not exist at all, and even if it must, evolutionary courses can be safer than our wild (relatively speaking) ride down the evolutionary NASCAR lane; we could crouch and freeze, like the emerald-blooded horseshoe crabs I used to kick back to the sea when they got beached, crabs unchanged since the Silurian, 400 million years ago. If there had to be mammals, we could be the blundering possum, the same now as it was in the age of the dinosaurs. If there's a principle of maximum diversity, there needs to be these insane stretches of the atom: planets with rings; jeweled tropical creatures like the peacock, the extravagant opposite of camouflage, because the easy tropics require that life stay pruned. There needs to be Kyle Andersons.

It is my idea that the principle of maximum diversity might apply to the neurological as well as to the more basic stuff of our lives, and since I wonder what Freeman Dyson would do with this notion, I diddle around and finally just write to him and ask him. He answers,

I agree with you that the same principle should also apply to neurology, when the science of neurology reaches the point where we understand how our brains work. We are not there yet. But I agree with you that Temple Grandin and others like her should be treasured and not genetically expunged. Another example is our friend Sabriye Tenberken, a blind lady who runs a school for blind children in Tibet and is now launching a new international organization called Braille Without Borders. Sabriye is indignant when anyone calls her handicapped. She says, "I am not handicapped—I am privileged. If I did not have the advantage of being blind, I would never have achieved so much."

If we are meant, or sentenced, to be infinite in all directions, then I guess neurodiversity must happen also, a schizophrenic or bipolar or Tourettic occurring at first here and there and dying out because of shunning or bad choices or simply lack of a breeding partner. There is an australopithecine male, short and hairy as all pre-humans, who unaccountably foams in terror at the frogs his companions eat, or stares at the rings in rocks. The females regard him with irritation and do not present him their backsides. End of story. But not for God, for whom the unfolding of possibility forms the one temptation, and who moves like resistless dream logic through our atoms. And who pushes that australopithecine intelligence along until one day it says, Let me invent chemicals for these people. Let me see if the chemicals work at making them act normal, or at least more normal, and maybe in the process I'll make some money. Let me put lead and mercury into the drinking water, and we'll worry about the delicate neurological processes later. And somehow there are more of these people, in a kind of chemical camouflage sometimes, and backsides do get presented and there are more and more of them. And they begin to talk to one another, about things like fear of frogs.

In one sense Kyle Anderson's a genetic horror story, the kind David Comings outlined in *The Gene Bomb*. The book argues that the world now practices "unnatural selection," medicating those with ADHD, bipolar disorder, multiple personalities, Tourette's (Comings's specialty is treating Touretics), so they can reproduce and grow in number. With Kyle, it's a matter of interpretation how much you want to relate those two things—the killing and the ADHD—or if you want to reach for the scribbled note about schizoid affective disorder, or dismiss both. But it's hard to shake the response that a boy who would do that is neuroatypical, crazy as only human beings can become. In a sense, though, Kyle showed the methodical forethought of an Adolf Eichmann, the Nazi war criminal whose trial—detailing days of monitoring train schedules for concentration camps and generating death-camp paperwork—caused Hannah Arendt to coin the term *the banality of evil*. Kyle's a monster, but in the narrative of his defense attorney, at least, a banal monster. He had taken apart VCRs, fish-pond filters, toasters. He was interested in the mechanics of things. The next stage in the clinical and almost mechanical task he'd set for himself was the human body. Or perhaps.

I'm not sure whether to assign all of him to the category of evolutionary aberration—Jack the Ripper–type monster—or to assign some of him to the category of evolutionary logic, the get-the-right-tools, get-the-job-done, and don't-look-beyond-the-job quality that seems so typical of us. Such human qualities: taskorientedness. Surplus killing. I want to say: learning how the hell things work. Perhaps it is our hell at times: made in God's image, we share that restless intelligence.

The two attorneys narrate different versions of the story of Kyle. One has a plaintively human quality, with the strange twist of not recognizing the difference between a human child and a toaster. One is unimaginable. And condemns me, I think.

BEFORE MY DIAGNOSIS as manic-depressive in my late twenties, I'd been called everything from depressed to schizophrenic, which was, if you'll pardon the pun, crazy: manic-depressive poster girl that I was. If you'd met me, reader, you probably could have diagnosed me yourself. I tried suicide in between bouts of partying and weird flamboyance: I walked to receive my college diploma in a vintage satin evening gown and a rhinestone choker and inexplicably wrote to *The Wall Street Journal,* telling them they should write stories about me. Twice friends stopped me from marrying men I had met the same night. I can feel my brain within my skull sometimes, the way you feel your heart thudding in your chest, as if it's trying to evolve into something else, or perhaps has been filled with pins. It's a noisy, busy place, my head, at least some of the time.

Right now my mind's in a phase of furiously narrating in a *you* voice: you'd better put that back in the refrigerator, you need to try to sleep now. It's kind of irritating, like having a mad mother on the inside of your ear. It doesn't bother me much, any more than a cat who won't stop meowing might. Minds, in my experience, are messy, loud places. The other night I sat and remembered some disagreements—nothing to the point of argument—with people I'd had that day, throwing in things I could have said the way you do, when I suddenly remembered a violent disagreement between two people one of whom declared he never wanted to see the other one again. I couldn't place it for the life of me, then I realized it had happened entirely between two people in my head. *Really, folks,* I found myself thinking, *can't you at least keep it among yourselves?*

My friend Dawn's written a book, called *Songs of the Gorilla Nation: My Journey Through Autism.* I read it very early on and loved it. One day I browse her Amazon.com book site, procrastinating, when I find this reader's comment: "With all due respect to the author's incredible journey, she is in reality a very different kind of human being and I have trouble placing her in my experience. . . . I have trouble with the reality she is describing and often 'how' she is describing . . . it has an alien quality."

How strange to think of Dawn and me and all of our kin as aliens, as a different kind of human being, as if we've branched off like Neanderthals, or the hominids who lived 18,000 years ago and were nicknamed the hobbit people. And it opens up the question of how many languages consciousness speaks, one for each individual or, as this Amazon reviewer seems to think, just two. And which conforms most closely to sanity and health.

Paul Collins, father of an autistic son, wrote this about his boy:

> Autistics are described by others—and by themselves—
> as aliens among humans. But there's an irony to this, for
> precisely the opposite is true. They are us, and to understand
> them is to begin to understand what it means to be human.

Think of it: a disability is usually defined in terms of what is missing. A child tugs at his or her parents and whispers, "Where's that man's arm?" But autism is an ability and a disability: it is as much about what is abundant as what is missing, an overexpression of the very traits that make our species unique. Other animals are social, but only humans are capable of abstract logic. The autistic outhumans the humans, and we can scarcely recognize the result.

You could argue that bipolar disorder, too, outhumans the human, living so fully those human qualities of joy and grief. As one bipolar writes on a Web support group, "Everything influences us." Manic-depressives Vincent van Gogh, Sylvia Plath, Georgia O'Keeffe, Blake, Rossini—ironically, the artists people are least likely to find incomprehensible. It may be that the hyperbole of this disease—something I recognized in myself even as a child—leaves a clearer imprint when displayed artistically, like the leaping out of van Gogh's suns and skies. But I'm afraid I may be trying to defend myself from my own monstrosity, the chance that I, like the young man I saw lowercased from personhood, represent a human coughing all over the progress of evolution.

THROUGHOUT AND AFTER the trial this thought—my relationship to Kyle—eats at me. Stendhal's proved no help. I find myself pulling out my old preteen and teenage diaries, facing the girl who lived as Kyle's counterpart, at least in some senses: the one I've mentally seated next to him, at the table behind the wooden bar that separates the guilty and the judging from the innocent. I should say at the outset that my memory of these years is sketchy and so I feel, entering these diaries, as if I'm encountering someone distinct from me in a lot of ways: like meeting someone you knew well at a time like grammar school, where the context for your knowing has not just passed but passed in an irretrievable way. It's less memory than judgment. You look for resemblances; you sum her up.

Here's that young girl's background. My great-grandmother, from Barbados, seems to have been bipolar. I didn't know her, but all the fragments I know of her point that way—her promiscuity and compulsive spending, hurting and abandoning her children, the recollections of everyone who lived with her on Barbados. She left behind a chaotic life and fourteen children, some of whom also seemed to have suffered from various mental disorders, several dying tragically, one at her hands when she forced him to scrub floors when he had pneumonia. One married a man in Martinique and died by poison, supposedly administered by his mother. Her depressive son, my grandfather, rarely spoke. Her great-grandchildren have carried on the legacy, many of us bearing this disorder.

All this came before me, and with me, but remained largely unknown to me until adulthood. My family did not speak of mental illness. If we mentioned my great-grandmother, she generally fell under the heading of "a character" or, if the speaker wanted to be unusually forthcoming, "not all she should be." We referred to my grandfather as an insomniac and a "man of few words."

I say all this to point out that when I began keeping a diary, my chronic examinations of my own mental illness were, however clumsy, not instilled by anything around me, but flowed from my own head.

I KEPT MY EARLIEST DIARY at the age of eleven, in 1968. It was the year after the Summer of Love, when my father would sometimes entertain us by taking us for a drive to Greenwich Village in New York—we lived about ten or fifteen miles away in urban New Jersey—to "see the hippies." We drove around and around, gawking at them as if they were in a zoo, at all the things that seemed bizarre and otherworldly enough to make them a destination point: scruffy bell-bottoms, beads and peace sign necklaces, long hair, and the rare and exotic sighting of armpit hair on young, nonimmigrant women. I had beads called "love beads" back then, reserved for special events, and white lipstick, and even a paper minidress. (Paper clothing came and went fast, though at the time we thought it would be the norm someday.) I used the word *groovy* a lot in my diary, and *fabby*. I spent most of my time worrying about lipstick, nail polish, my hair that wouldn't straighten, pimples, and boys.

Nevertheless, every couple of days something off crept in. My hands shook; they seem to have been the bane of my existence, and I cried uncontrollably, at things both good and bad. I went blank and lost small but scary bits of time. At school, my extreme "daydreaming" brought me to the point where I noted I often "lost touch with reality," and someone had to be assigned every day to poke me in the back when I seemed to be drifting away.

At thirteen I wrote:

Today Mom left $5.00 on the kitchen table & it completely disappeared! She's convinced I took it, but I don't remember even touching it. So many things have been disappearing lately. I'm so afraid I'm mentally ill. There are times when I just seem to blank out. God, I'm so scared.

The next day I described the clock in my room being rearranged after a short period of blankness. ("I almost died. I don't know if its me or what.")

At age eleven I tried to describe the oscillations of my moods:

"A" mood is my regular mood. When I am in a B mood I love everything—practically. I am sentimental, and I kind of (well, not *kind of*—*do*) want to cry at the wonderful life God has ready. [I'm reproducing these entries as accurately as I can; I wrote words I wanted to be italicized sharply canted to the right.]

This was an entry in my first diary, and after making it, I started noting from time to time whether the entry I wrote came from "A" or "B." I didn't have a designation for depression but felt that, too, and voiced a great deal of confusion about its intensity. "I can't explain this misery I'm in. I'm psychic—maybe it's a premonition of things to come," I wrote once. I suppose all kids this age get moody, hormonal, intense. I don't have clear ways of judging what might be normal, or neurotypical, except that my blanking out seems to have been real, chronic, and noticeable to everyone around me, as was my inability at times to stop crying. I know that I had formulated suicide plans by eleven—a bottle of extra-strength Excedrin, which a friend told me would kill you for sure—and also mentally decorated the interior of my first apartment, down to each piece of furniture, and the colors and patterns of the window decor and the rugs. I had the prolixity of the bipolar writer, like an immature version of Plath with her poem a day; I mentioned that I'd just finished a novel, several plays, songs, and a handful of poems on what seemed like a bi-weekly basis (one quality I wish had outlasted time and medicine). I prayed constantly, believed in God, and accepted the doctrine of reincarnation.

Today I don't want to say much. I'm all confused & I don't know—I just don't know. I keep terrifying myself by imagining that I got my ESP from the Devil & he's going to claim my soul for it when I die. And something way down deep inside me keeps kicking up & being rebellious & demanding something & I don't know what it wants.

I hit on these themes over and over: God controlled the movements of my cat and sent me messages through her; alternation between a sense of ecstasy and damnation: *I think I may be possessed.* When I wrote at twelve "I feel as if I don't know myself," the statement comes less as preteen drama and confusion than as a factual statement of defeat, after days of feeling soaked in the joy I called my "good stomachache," pouring out poems, plays, and novels, then days where I couldn't stand the barest elements of my life. Days when my limbs disgusted me, my bowels. I divided myself up, earlier that year, into three people: Sue, who was reckless and impulsive; Suzanne, cautious and a writer and thinker; Suzie, a "mischievous imp." And I signed my diary accordingly.

"Am I, I wonder, schizophrenic?" I asked myself. And I would say perhaps my Dr. L. lit onto something if I wasn't misinformed at the time about the definition of schizophrenia.

By age eleven I judged myself, on the same questions I consider now. Some of the time I believed myself not just mentally ill but evil. I didn't say why, and at this remove I don't know why. I know that the reasons I give as I spill out those fears are all internal: the "something" inside, the sense of sharpened mental powers. Occasionally I wrote something more bizarre:

> Sometimes I think that maybe Earth is an experiment created by scientists on some other world, or Mom, Dad, Chris & everyone else is in some hideous conspiracy against me!

Or, later, at fifteen:

> Sometimes I think I'm OK, but other times I think I'm really sick. Like yesterday, I got very very mad at Alice [a friend], and I was sitting alone in her living room, and the anger was just building and building inside me. All of a sudden tears were running down my cheeks & I was hitting myself really hard with a hairbrush.

My consciousness fueled enough, no doubt terrible, literary work to equal in pages several adult careers; it kept saved mice squittering in basement cages and fed little Socrates, whom, I wrote, "I wrapped in tissue . . . he looked just like a little nun." And my mind terrified me as well, with its clamors, its swells and rages, its autonomy from anything I could identify as mine.

I did not write in my diary every day; maybe I'd know more if I did. But I doubt it. I think I'd have a few more glimpses like those above and lots more information on acne products with names like Propa pH; lipsticks with names like Frosted Cocoa Mocha. Part of the reason I pose this girl—surly, I imagine, in her defendant's chair, and confused—is that she has created this distance as much as time or my own choices have.

Let me be clear. It's not that I want to know her or possess her in any way: I could say of her, if she were a man, "Of all men else I have avoided thee," as Macbeth said of Macduff. I opened these journals in middle age, and then with a feeling that the person within repulsed me, or would repulse me. (Typing the Macbeth quote above, I mistyped, the first time, "Of all men else I have avoided me.") I thought I didn't want to see her older, drug-addled, writing things like "heroin & LSD [together] are my two favorite his [highs]," and mentioning, at the end of a long entry about trying to cop a dime bag of pot, the bloody battles of my friends. I don't even say why Kevin tried to stab John-John, his best friend, to death. It sounds as though in the world I was in, that outcome would always make a certain kind of sense, a problem for someone who already had enough problems, the way now I might respond to a friend having a bout with asthma.

I hate that girl. I have negative self-talk about her, as an old therapist would say, and she makes me cringe. When she came down off the astonishing amount of drugs she used, she became suicidal.

"I feel so bad, I swear I want to die," I wrote again and again. And I tried to, in the dainty way of women. At fourteen I swallowed a bottle of Quaaludes but I hollered as I passed out and then spent three days in the hospital.

But what surprises me now: the little one scares me more. Even with the silky innocence of her love beads and stabs at lipstick. She had no heroin or LSD or barbiturates to explain her. She simply had bouts of paranoia and depression and ecstasy and waiting for the devil to come and claim her soul. Or she wrote a novel. She simply lived a neurodiverse life: possible, but not easy.

MY JOURNALS are always written with an odd sense of audience. I called it various things—Diary, Cindy one year, Paper, or once, "Dear Whatever The Fuck U Are." Whatever I called this entity I wrote in, I looped around it a lot of the time, or beat my pen against it. I treated it as distinct; I had encounters with it. ("Pray for me," I asked my diary once.) "I'm trying to explain this in a way you'll understand," I'd write, or "I'm trying to make this clear to you, though it probably won't make sense." Once a month or so I wrote an entry that was a deliberate silence, an allusion to something I wouldn't say: "I won't go into it now, Cin, I don't want to talk about it." "I don't want to tell you about this," I said at points elsewhere. The paper had become a transparent medium through which I saw something that could not handle the burden of my thoughts.

Even if it was only myself. Myself later that week, or after thirty-five years. Who else could it be? I had judged myself correctly, it seems. I found sections in my journals, maybe two or three per writing year, where pages had been ripped out without any care, tattered edges with faint pen strokes visible. I did that. I do vaguely remember doing that. And I remember that I didn't do that self-editing as a child but as an adult, starting about ten years ago.

Bruce says, "You didn't want Jin to ever see it." But I remember my first tearings, long before Jin: I didn't want to see them again myself. And now I have no idea what they said. If that forgetfulness is a mental block, then it's worked. I've become my own Rosemary Woods. I've rejected that girl, and she, as if she knew my capacity for this, danced sometimes around what she would tell me.

"MY BODY IS DEAD," Orestes tells Menelaus in the *Oresteia*, when he has killed his mother and lies pursued by the Furies. "I am the name it had."

I gotta quit doing <u>heroin</u> & <u>LSD</u> but I can't they're my 2 favorite his. I wish I had a cool steady boyfriend. Woo, I can't believe I can write—I'm tripping so heavy & feeling very weird & hi. Tonite at the King [Burger King, a hangout] everything was red & blue esp. the woodwork. I was cracking up over the pig. I'm sick—I know only a few people who could stand to do as much drugs as I can all at once— one's Kevin Conway—look how he ended up. . . . I <u>love</u>

heroin & LSD together plus pot & downs & a little beer—
it's my favorite hi.

I wrote this entry on January 13, noting that I'd tripped fifteen times since Christmas, pretty much every day. LSD domi-
nates this one journal; at this age half-used school notebooks—the
old tan ones—served as diaries, so I wrote and drew all over the
plain covers. I also stuck a page of drawings on the bottom of this
entry, all spirals and sketches of eyes: pupils slit and staring, under
lashes or brows also thick and straight, or thick and pinworm-
squiggly. I had been leaning with all my weight into the pen. Lyrics
from Alice Cooper, the shock rocker who wore Gothic makeup
and sang about blood and death and mental institutions, lace the
margins of the pages and the covers of the book.

I REREAD THESE DIARY ENTRIES in late summer, thinking
about buying Jin's things for the new school year. Then I snap on
the TV and see none other than Alice Cooper; he's doing com-
mercials for Staples, advertising back-to-school supplies. He does
the commercial in full Goth makeup and with his little daughter,
or some child actress posing as his daughter. I read later that
though he still performs, he's willing to admit to what a regular
guy he is; he golfs, goes to church, coaches soccer teams.

This girl—who called herself a "halfway junkie" at fifteen—
reincarnates that eleven- and twelve-year-old. She's someone else,
different, someone who takes insane risks, not just in the drugs
she uses but in things like sleeping under a gun, hanging out with
armed paranoid speed freaks, hitchhiking everywhere and get-

ting into the car no matter who stopped, so that at least once she had to jump out while it was moving. She did what she wanted. She came and went. Her handwriting, scrawling to the right, differs from the careful upright of that young girl. Still it seems clear that the young one's panics over conspiracies, the demons, the novels that had to be written *now*, led her to her second existence, with its deep chemical lulls.

What could have been worse than the records I kept? Where I equate myself with Kevin Conway, the Kyle Anderson of my world. Me = Kevin = Kyle Anderson. I have lost any sight of the evolutionary reason for myself, other than to be hammered pharmacologically into the space of the normal.

The first time I spoke to Dawn Prince-Hughes, we sat together at a playground. Our young sons slid and hung on the playground equipment, and discovered each other over a collection of Jin's Matchbox cars. Somehow in that seemingly infinite downtime of young motherhood, we looked at each other and started talking and talked, after the first minute, with a strange frankness, as if we knew to take some layers off.

Dawn said, about the increasing number of autistics, "It's like society's making us, like they need us, you know? Lint filters for all the shit that's out there."

Reading all these journals, I lose a sense of mission. If I'm filtering anything, it's stuck, it's ceased to pass.

IN *THE GENE BOMB*, David Comings has all kinds of schemes for protecting the world from the likes of me. Easier access to abortion, incentives for early reproduction by the neurotypical and intelligent. But in the decade since he wrote this book, the proliferation of the atypicals continued: autism increasing at the rate of 20 percent a year, according to the U.S. Department of Health. Perhaps we've lost the battle and the war. Our human DNA pool is tiny. About 100,000 years ago, give or take some millennia, we faced a population bottleneck that reduced our number to as little as 10,000. A Harvard scientist, Maryellen Ruvolo, figured this out by tracing back our DNA. Our pool now remains so small you and I, whoever and wherever you are, are more alike than any two mountain gorillas living in the same tribe in Africa. Now those abnormal genes like autism and hyperactivity, if they are genes, bloom along the stem of this freakishly singular genome.

> *When you see your likeness, you rejoice. But when you see*
> *your image which came into existence before you, which*
> *neither dies nor is manifested, how much will you endure?*
>
> —THE GNOSTIC GOSPEL OF THOMAS

I drink coffee with Ned Markosian, a colleague, a presentist philosopher, who argues that only present objects can be said to exist. How, I ask him, does being a presentist affect your life? He's drinking one of those drinks that seems more like a milk shake than coffee, with cream on top.

"I think it informs the way things seem to me," he says. "To the extent it does, it's a little bit sad. When I used to think about past people or past things I could just think, They're no longer present." He had a dog he loved named Shün, he tells me, a labby mutt, and Shün died. "I used to think all kinds of things about him.

I could make all sorts of propositions about him, like that Shün was a good dog, I loved Shün. As a presentist, when his body went out of existence, I could no longer make propositions about him that implied his existence." Ned contemplates, finishes his milky drink, and then the creamy coffee never was. "I couldn't say Shün was a good dog anymore."

Ned explains that now he can only make general propositions about the dog, using a phrase like "There was a dog named Shün," because in some sense the sentence structure implies it could be any dog, a fictional dog, not his Shün, the patched dog whose wet nose probably woke Ned in the morning, if we could say he existed.

Ned does look sad about this, trapped in the spaces the language of his philosophy allows him. Part of me's dying to ask, What if it were your children? Would you be willing to bury even them, as hypothetical children? I'm no presentist and could never do that. Though my life in front of me in the form of diary pages comes square by square, discrete, with no sense of things flowing from one moment toward its future moment; it's like seeing the stills of a movie. On August 7, 1972, I wrote, "I really wish I had someone to love me, I mean really love me, over everyone else." Exactly ten years later I married. But the irony, or beauty, of the coincidence has no depth; the woman who married has, again, not fulfilled this dead one but left her behind, a general proposition.

I SUPPOSE I exist in a line with these earlier female humans, these diary keepers, like an evolutionary tree, with a touch of what Jung would call "race memory." We share a common nervous system; we're all manic-depressives. I'm medicated now. I don't often remember what it feels like to be suicidal, and while I'm manic from time to time, and depressed, I don't conjure up devils. But I would not choose ever to become overmedicated or to leave my tribe. I like my mind the way it is, like a striving city, or a small town at least, noisy and architectural. I want to believe there is value in this, and in my beautiful friends. Somehow, Kyle Anderson in his shapeless body has come along as a rebuke: my ability to kill him, my ability to be him.

When I hear the judge say at sentencing, "I wish we had a medicine to test for people like you," though it's lack of empathy he means, I hear that comment expand to mean me. And now that there's gene testing and gene correcting, the possibility's become real.

I check in with my online tribe to see how many of them would want to be bipolar again. One man writes:

> I choose not to look at bipolar as an illness at all. In fact, I couldn't imagine myself as not being bipolar, nor would I want to be. The bipolar is a strong componant [sic] of who I am, and I do not wish to be anyone else but me.
>
> It aggravates me that bipolar mania and hypomania abilities/attributes are looked at as not the abilities of the individual, but as a sickness that has nothing to do with the individual; what could be more dehumanizing? Isn't that being deprived of oneself?

"Mental illness understood is truly a way to happiness," writes a woman named Maria, though others see it as a curse. "I feel, and cause others to feel," says one bipolar. "Touched, the life of the imagination is the real life."

"Look at how normals live and treat each other," says a man named Harry, wanting no part of that.

WE SEEM to be heading to a brave new world. Authors like Kate Hayles call this the "post-human era." Human DNA's been inserted into a cow egg; human organs live in pigs; and a human ear, bred for transplant, turns deaf to the heavens as it grows inside the back of a mouse. We've mapped the human genome and debate what to do with that knowledge, with experimentation springing up here and there. A company in British Columbia called Chromos Molecular Systems has developed artificial chromosomes. Artificial chromosomes could conceivably be strung together to create an artificial human, or at least a human who could mate only with other humans created from the same manufactured chromosomes. This would be another form of speciation. And I can't imagine anyone—not the molecular engineers manipulating these minute blueprints, not the anxious parents seeing only babies—putting into the blueprints the codes for autism or bipolar disorder or whatever else resembles me.

A less drastic and more likely outcome will be manipulating the genome as it appears, adding and removing some of the genes that, singly or together, cause what we collectively view as trouble. Whether that will be a bad thing or a good thing remains to be seen; any guessing I can do either way would be self-serving. It seems ironic, though, for the neurodiverse to identify themselves and insist on the right to their culture even as medicine evolves to-ward finding those mind ways an erasable smudge on the genome.

Freeman Dyson writes to me, "The real problem with neu-rodiversity is that if parents are given a free choice they will not want it. Hardly any parents will want a child who will be men-tally abnormal."

WE ARGUE the genetic-manipulation question a lot with our friend Thor, a paleontologist who studies new technologies. We're talking one night, in another friend's kitchen, leaning on her butcher-block table, about zygote screening and genetic manipu-lation of our children. Would we choose only perfect children? Perfect in the eyes of whom? Our culture? Bruce and Thor taught a class that included the topic of genetic engineering. Thor al-lowed his students to do a hypothetical zygote, or prebirth, screen-ing. A majority who screened (not everyone in this class of seventy chose to) picked the male child, tall, with a high IQ and a good physique. This was the good bonny bairn our students yearned for.

Thor gave them a follow-up, at my request, with a chance to enable a "creativity gene," which he posited would give the child a greater-than-50-percent chance of increased creativity, but also a greater chance of being manic-depressive and addictive. Inter-estingly, slightly more than half the students chose this gene. I wonder if the choice has to do with the way the gene is packaged—as the creativity gene, not the crazy gene. Somehow, I don't imagine the future's genetic doctors presenting it that way in their counseling sessions.

We talk about this in the kitchen. I'm surprised to hear, as we talk about turning that gene on or off like flipping the kitchen light, Thor say whatever stable, normal genes there were he would give to his own child.

"Wouldn't you want her just to be who she was?"

"No." Thor's so positive that, for a minute, he makes me think.

As things stand in our genetically sloppy world, Thor has a daughter named Laura he loves as much as anyone has ever loved a daughter, and I know he's not voting this way because of something Laura lacks.

He says, "I'd just want my child to have what it takes to be happy," and I have to admit I want this, too. When I say yes to all these things, it's myself I'm talking about, allowing myself to live.

PETER WARD WRITES of us humans, in *Future Evolution*, that we are "mankind, the consummate weed." He also writes that humans now practice "unnatural selection," with the mentally unstable proliferating, so I guess I'm a weed among weeds. And perhaps the technology to eradicate my kind of weed will win out in the next hundred years or so, and we'll contract the directional infinity of the human mind, even as we teach language to apes and expand the range of their consciousness.

WHEN I GO TO MY CHURCH—we used to call it the Funeral Church, and now it's the Karate Church—I confess to being a sinner, one among other sinners, it's true, but "of whom I am the chief." And this is true for so many reasons: because my mind,

standing and singing for over an hour, is on the muffins; because
I'm a thorn on the genome; because I lived as a bad child and a
bad young girl and because, having done so, I dissect those girls
away, though they aggressively cry out to me; because even I cannot love them, though they're my parents and my children.

In August the sun gets so bright it snaps the irids like a rubber band, and the church's interior is white. The sparring
dummy's hung with its seraphic sheet. We're not worrying about
dead people anymore, just, in Barbara's case, hobnobbing with
them if they happen to come around.

My friend Rosina, bless her, once said of my diaries, "They
were your one link with the world. You were saving yourself." I
don't believe her. Or perhaps we all record things like *I can't believe I can write—I'm tripping so heavy & feeling very weird & hi* or
even just *it's sunny out for a change* to try to outrun the insistent pre-
sentism of the universe, because life, however we live it, is unbe-
lievable. Nothing outlasts, Ned tells me, its material extinction.
And the body each decade regenerates itself and all I had was
paper, a white drowning.

What shall we do with the time before supper?
Perhaps see the madwomen with their pretty songs.

FOUCAULT WRITES that in the 1800s the great London Bethlehem Hospital for the Insane, the place known as Bedlam, opened its doors every Sunday and collected a penny from Londoners who arrived in their high-waisted dresses and tight vests, their pushed-up sleeves and brooches filled with the stiff hair of their dead, to come in and regard the insane. The hospital made 400 pounds a year at this to supplement, presumably, the crusts their lunatics begged out windows, happy I guess to discover the openhandedness of the public's "mocking laughter and insulting pity," as a doctor of the time wrote. Foucault called the practice "one of the Sunday distractions for the Left Bank bourgeoisie," who loaded up on their Sunday drops of opium and strolled through Bedlam as if it were a zoo.

Society, as Foucault writes in *Madness and Civilization*, has a large stake in the mad. We serve as foil, entertainment, "glorified scandal," and objects of a kind of ultimate dread, since human culture rests so heavily on its sense of the mind.

Oddly enough when I imagine this scene, in Bedlam, I use the point of view of the visitor—regarding men and women tied, filthy, and babbling—rather than as one of the viewed, though I'm a bedlamite and would have been there, had I lived then.

"You were crazy," one of my college professors said to me, meeting up with me later in life, remembering, I guess, black satin, grief, near-marriages. Who knows what. "And I mean really crazy."

Well, I was. But that's not the story I want to tell, so I'll leave my old bedlams where they lie. I'm medicated now and so not that kind of crazy anymore. I can't help feeling implicated by Foucault, and by his Bedlam.

But I don't want, in writing, to put myself into that zoo. I want to say: this is another way to be human.

I OFTEN MEET DAWN at a coffee shop called Stuart's, full of overstuffed and slightly rotting furniture. The floor is a mass of crumbs; as a baby my son would graze on it if I didn't yank him up. Students love this place and hang out here with their laptops and equations and depressing novels, all the things we see fit to cram into their heads. Some of our downtown itinerants come, nursing coffee or handfuls of jellybeans from a vending machine.

A few years back, the two men who came to be known as the Beltway Snipers—John Mohammed and Lee Malvo—came here every day, playing chess. After a spring and summer in Bellingham, they went on to the Maryland and D.C. area, where they shot thirteen people in three weeks, from the back of an old car they modified with a rifle hole. Across the street from us stands the old Waterfront Tavern, a place that will acquire the nickname Serial Killer Café, since Mohammed, Malvo, Ted Bundy, and Kenneth Bianchi have all hung out there, drinking the Waterfront's dollar mugs of beer.

Mohammed and Malvo form, perhaps, bookends to us, Dawn with her long blond dreadlocks and grand presence, me a little comical I think, always putting my clothes on inside out or forgetting it's not seemly to wear pants splitting at the crotch. John Mohammed and Lee Malvo sit calm and still at the chess table, two minds pouring themselves out on the movements of wooden pieces, knight to king two. Next to them always lies a green duffel bag; Mohammed even takes it to the restroom, clanking all the way. It's the rifle, clanking out the deaths it contains, just as the knights glide across the board holding their checkmates and defeats. When the pair talk it's in low tones, solemn and quiet. Since they go from Bellingham to Maryland, presumably they're planning here this job they've decided to do. They will write a note to the police. Please Call Me God, they'll say, asking for $10 million to stop the shooting.

Dawn and I have our own job to do, I think. We want to put our minds in context; it's a job that began the first day we met.

"I can only tell you images," Dawn says when I ask her things, like what she sees as death. "It's a cloud, a huge cloud, and it's traveling up like this," and she gestures with her hands.

"Is that the soul?"

"I don't know. I don't know if I believe in the soul. I just see the cloud and this is what it's doing, going up."

One day Dawn said to me, "I wonder how other people can not *feel* things." She always sees a mental loop of a golden retriever being hit by a car, something she'd witnessed years before. I had been telling her about my head full of rooms and characters who flit in and out of them, some clear and some not. I had just seen a little girl, all bloody, being locked away and told with surprising compassion not to come out again.

Six months later the snipers will be ruled sane and competent to stand trial. Their motives never come entirely into focus, whether it's something to do with Mohammed's sympathy for the Nation of Islam or greed or an elaborate plot to kill Mohammed's ex-wife or all of the preceding. John Mohammed will take over his own defense for a while, politely questioning the police officers who once questioned him at the scene of the shootings.

"Did my story make sense?" he asks a policeman who saw him lurking near a downed truck driver.

All these minds form part of the tangled web we wove, 50,000 years ago, when, as neurobiologist William Calvin (author of *A Brain for All Seasons, A Brief History of the Mind,* and other books) believes, we humans coordinated tossing our javelins and somehow formed the neurological skeins of modern consciousness.

WE HAVE no more zoolike Bedlams so our *lunatics*—not a word in much use anymore—haunt movies and TV, stalking people, boiling rabbits in cooking pots. We love to watch them still, me, too, though I'm one of the implicated. The popular madman used to be someone like Anthony Perkins in *Psycho*, a schizophrenic turning his head to become his murderess mother; he encompassed some weird social creepiness about duality, the split mind. Now schizophrenia has a much more sophisticated and nuanced definition, and I see the culture using the manic-depressive to hold this fear. Recently I saw a manic boy shoot up his school on a cop show and, on another channel, a bipolar woman stalk her ex-boyfriend. Cultures worry about the deviant. The gene bomb, Comings thinks, clicks fearfully in its missile of flesh. Anthropologist Peter Ward worries in *Future Evolution* about the effect of "the children that in another age would die early, but here will live and even breed, and in some cases perpetuate their disabilities."

Darwinian evolution sees our brain progressing toward a cerebral and unitary consciousness—the jewel on the evolutionary chain. Shatter the jewel on the chain and it fractures: shards flying outward and inward. Such a common symptom of lunacy, to feel fragments in the brain.

Certain things, like the feeling of pins in the brain, come with mania, along with the sense of overwhelming mental noise, voices. I have people in my head who seem to exist in some sense apart, words that perseverate and feel planted, like tape recordings, by someone else. Or like the crooning of a vinyl record with dings in the groove. What sticks its finger in my little song? *Lunacy* is there now, and though it seems there must be some chord or lyric beyond that word, we never get there, never pass this one singing. *Lunacy, lunacy:* so sweet, so beautiful: a moth in it, a moon, a tug of water. I find myself shaking my head sometimes, as if I might dislodge it all. (A man on a message board I belong to talks about numbers "falling out of his head.") And though it sounds strange, it doesn't really bother me; I know when the noise grows beyond my control and have a medication regimen to follow—more gabapentin, tranquilizers if necessary—and I meditate, finding the strands that say *this is a passing thing.*

I think I'm possessed by the devil, I wrote in my diary when I was ten.

I don't think that anymore, though I can't help wondering how it would be to be one of those exhibits, if without medication or anyone to listen to me I'd fall apart and do things amusing to see. Raw sewage poured into these old Bedlams, and enormous rats; women's corpses were dragged out dead of rat bite. Darkness, whips, and chain or rope restraints constituted treatment. I might turn wildly out of my wits. Or I might be in my wits some of the time, since they took you based on your worst moments. I would like to think Dawn, who'd be there, would be my friend, and we who are both so obsessed with animals would find sentience in the deadly sequins of the rats' eyes.

OUTSIDE IT'S THE NIGHT of a lunar eclipse and the moon's a ruddy thumbnail. Jin's at a friend's and Bruce, our friend Thor, and I run into the street, looking to see that oystery roundness in shadow; we live so far west the eclipse totality occurs at a little after five, and so the full moon rises in umbra, the earth a round veil leaving the shadowed part of the moon visible but dark, bricky, like the real hunk of dirt that it is. No poet's moon this, no pearl, no watery luna. Rather, it's a mirror of sorts: not of our physical features but our planetary bulk. We're the huge globe dragging the catastrophe of our shadow across a piece of rock a quarter million miles away. As we slide all the way over, the moon's normalcy reemerges in wedges bright as the edge of a dime.

Thor keeps joking, Look! I can see the shadow of your house up there! and I almost feel like I can. It's nauseating somehow, this exhalation of our solidity.

It makes me wonder why the moon's the keeper of lunacy, by word derivation its namesake and terrestrial daughter. Is it that it changes, every month, from a bright cradle to a face and back again? Or that we can't look at the sun for long, and the planets and stars remain as small as lamps or candles, but the moon—its pocked size, hovering like the eye of our darkness—confirms our embodiment, as an earth, as a people on an earth? A lunifying thought.

A few days after the eclipse a woman, middle-aged, with a huge bruise on the left side of her face that radiates from her eye across her cheekbone, comes up to Bruce and me while we buy groceries. We wheel mindlessly down the bread, spice, and coffee aisle and it smells like a modern alchemist's lab, someone brewing rye and yeast and five-spice powder and Sumatran. Jin's eating baked Sun Chips.

I'm looking, she says, for people who believe eating healthy food allows God to come into your brain. Her middle-aged face jowling, pulled by gravity; she has pale, thin hair. The reddening veils her shiny face into partial eclipse, a strange rhyme with the day before.

A musician we know stops to say hi and she addresses him, too. Do you believe in eating healthy food? Yes, he says. His manner is always very kind and calm. Do you know angels are appearing here? she wants to know.

That's fine, he tells her, kindly.

Angels have been appearing in the Food Coop lately, she says. She doesn't seem able to stop talking: There are more angels here in the coop than in church. You know who they are by their bright healthy faces. Junk food keeps God out of our brains. Eat vegetables. And so on and so on.

David the musician keeps saying, That's fine. That's fine really.

She was a little wacky, we tell Jin later.

I like her, he says, out of his bright healthy face.

> *In the bonnie cells of Bedlam*
> *Ere I was one-and-twenty*
> *I had hempen bracelets strong*
> *And merry whips, ding-dong*
> *And prayer and fasting plenty.*

I found this Walter Scott quote in an article written in 1844 by A. Brigham. He wrote for a magazine called *The American Journal of Insanity* and seems to have been not just the keeper of an asylum but a great fan of literature—Shakespeare and Scott in particular. Shakespeare created mad characters perfectly, he said, with the faithfulness of a physician, and Brigham knew this because of the resemblance of his patients to the people in the plays (he says this with a typical nineteenth-century love of typology, as if the insane draw from a limited pack of possibilities, like cards from a deck). It must be quite a life: Dr. Brigham wakes up in the morning and forks his rasher of bacon like a good gentleman, climbs into a carriage, and arrives at work, where his Ophelias press flowers onto all who pass, his Hamlets wrestle self-destruction, his Lears curse their young, and his Lady Macbeths wipe and wipe at their hands.

Canst thou not minister to a mind diseased? they might say, greeting him at the doorway. To which he could give Shakespeare's doctor's answer: Therein the patient must minister to himself.

I love Brigham. His tone's so human compared with the voice of modern medicine. Like his hero Samuel Johnson, Brigham believes everyone lives close to insanity. Though Brigham writes on the subject of literature, he can't stop harping on the need to avoid falling into lunacy: "Youth must not be passed in idleness, nor in reading romances and reveling in imaginary scenes of future happiness," he writes, urging instead "actual toil, manual labor." Fantasy opens before you like a hole you can't climb out of; you're an Alice with your distorted self waiting. Johnson, Brigham's hero, goes so far as to say that "if we speak with rigorous exactness, no human mind is in its right state" and writes movingly of the start of psychosis: "He who has nothing external that can divert him, must find pleasure in his own thoughts, and must conceive himself what he is not; for who is pleased with what he is?"

Who, indeed?

NEUROBIOLOGIST WILLIAM CALVIN, when I interviewed him at his home, defined our humanness as our ability to imagine "novel situations," the unreal or fantastic, though Brigham warns us not to allow ourselves this luxury of our species. Do we modern readers believe him? We tend to think of any experts writing before our time as cutely amusing, lost in the kindergarten of their antiquity. Yet our thinking is also quaint, ridiculous, of course. The future bends toward us like a blade.

I wonder about Dr. Johnson, and what Czeslaw Milosz wrote ("How many ways . . . do we discover the inaccessibility of another mind") about the icy-pure remoteness of another consciousness. I wonder if neurotypical and neuroatypical is another one of our culture's false divides. It may be that every consciousness is as crystalline and different, strange and faceted as a shard of glass. Maybe it's just the luck of the draw: I've spoken about pins and perseverations and satin gowns to doctors for whom these things are cues to reach for a prescription pad, secretly glad that they've never said these things aloud themselves.

MY GRANDFATHER, on the Italian side, was nervous. This word encapsulated his being toward the end of his life, and accounted for his unwillingness to do most things, like come out with us to a Chinese restaurant, or pay attention to his children and their lit-ter of fifteen grandchildren, many of whose names he could not tell you. He didn't leave his small, TV-cathode-lit apartment much, though he was healthy.

"He gets nervous," my mother said constantly of my grandfa-ther; we accepted it as the all-purpose engine of a life. My grand-father, called Pop-Pop by my cousins though I can't remember calling him anything, reacted with terror once when I said my car had broken down on the side of the road in a wealthy suburban New Jersey town, saying that anywhere you went these days, men waited on the side of the road to strip cars down to the chassis in broad day. He talked of muggers and burglars and diseases spread by cats, his world a bright festival of harm.

For most of my life my grandfather lived in south Florida, so I don't know if he spent his life nervous. Certainly the few times we drove down to see him he struck me as a jumpy guy, downing shot glasses of anisette and sitting in front of his layers and layers of caged parakeets, a wall of living noise he raised with nothing resembling love.

In spite of his nervousness, when he moved up north in his seventies, my grandfather let us tote him around sometimes. He liked going to the beach, and we occasionally took him to the ocean, where the surf frightened him but drew him anyway: he strode out a few feet into the water but then when a sudsy wave rose at him he held his hands up, saying *Stop, Stop* in terror.

There was a sea change, Foucault writes (if you'll pardon the pun) to the concept of the mad as spectacle from an earlier, more laissez-faire attitude, Tom O'Bedlams like a nomadic tribe. If the mad could be tolerated they were, and wandered around among the population, a part of Shakespeare's world, so that when he wanted to disguise his hunted character Edgar he had him dress as a "poor Tom"—Poor Tom stuck not just pins and nails but sprigs of rosemary, herb of remembrance, into his skin. My priest Father Joseph says our Jerusalem Orthodox church regarded its mad as an exercise in unconditional love, as well as a source of prophecy.

Since, I imagine, you'd want only so many people running around stuck with herbs like an Easter lamb, some European countries began the practice of turning their mentally ill over to boatmen, who promised to take them a certain distance away and sometimes carried a ship's worth of such cargo—floating, speculates Foucault, from port to port as unwanted as plague ships. It got lunatics out of the walled cities; it put the mad in the social place once occupied by lepers, now dwindled down to a few, and once kept, as Foucault writes, at a "sacred distance" from the culture. Often the ships' purpose was simply removal, but they also took the mad on pilgrimages to holy sites with cures specifically for the mind: at shrines like Saint-Hildebert de Gournay in France and Saint Dymphna at Gheel in Belgium. Of course, uncured lunatics didn't sail back to their homes, so villages like Gheel ended up forming colonies of the insane. Aside from where they sailed, the image of the ships became important: Foucault writes of the significance of water as symbol—the mad needed to be distanced but also purified, baptized almost. I think of them sent to the moon's element, water the one place on earth where another gravity slaps successfully against our own.

Sometimes in *Madness and Civilization* Foucault doesn't distinguish much between the lunatic and the drunkard, the gambler and the undifferentiated fool. Bosch's painting, *Ship of Fools,* has nuns, peasants, and a monk with a lute all crazily playing, a leaved tree with a death's-head on top for a mast, and a man vomiting off the bow. Several nude swimmers may have fallen over the side, and nobody looks bow-ward; the ship appears heading for a crash. A mockery of the pilgrimage of human life, say art critics: our belief in our own mastery while we live soft, debauched Boschian lives. "An illustrated allegory," says the WebMuseum, "the whole of mankind setting sail into the seas of time." Or what parts of itself mankind would release. I see myself and Dawn, N'Lili and

Kyle Anderson cupped in a leaking cockpit. I see John Mohammed and Lee Malvo waving good-bye.

MY MENTAL PEOPLE pop in and out and often become very clear to me if I have time to think. It's like a cocktail party. Gee, I really handled that, a biker guy will say of a conversation; he handles the tough stuff. If I have to have a sit-down with one of Jin's teachers or a colleague, he'll do it. A slightly prissy lady teaches. She goes over lessons and probably thinks about appropriate clothes to wear in the classroom, which isn't something the rest of them would give a rat's ass about. Cacophonous but not necessarily disturbing, just my own personal ship of fools. They're stereotypical to an extreme, my people (to a writer that's a bit disturbing, I have to admit), but however they came to be, it wasn't to populate a novel or a complex work of art. In their typicality lies their use.

And sometimes it's just those mental voices in the form of an echo of what I'm thinking, a persistent refrain (a *burden*, as refrain lines of a song used to be called), clearly chanted within the walls of my skull but just as clearly apart from the main thread qualifying as me, often just repeating what the self-narrative says—annoying to hear though it's usually something as simple as *buy butter buy butter and get the phone get the phone get the phone.*

Though I've had lots of medical help over the years, talking about voices has been something I've avoided with clinicians. It seems to get them worried—rooting around for prescription pads—or confused, though I understand the concept of repulsive inner voices and I don't have those, just, at times, annoying ones. It seems built in to psychiatry to distrust the burden—Freud lists vocal repetition as one of the elements of the uncanny, and the Greeks poured their discomfort at echolalia into the story of Echo, a silly nymph who blabbed something she shouldn't and got struck by Juno with the curse of meaningless repetition, so she could only say the last thing she heard again and again. Needless to say, she became quite creepy, and even the one she loved, Narcissus, ran from her. Though he was a lost cause anyway, always wondering at the strange reticence of the lovely, avid, lust-parched boy in the water.

MY GREAT-GRANDFATHER, the father of my nervous grandfather, set sail into the seas of time, coming here from a small village in Italy. He was an older man and wanted to work and send money home and then return to his village, a plan wrecked when his entire family back home died of cholera. He never learned English and therefore chose to remain for the rest of his life largely silent or misunderstood. He may have been nervous, too. He may have gone to his ship pursued by the matter pouring unchecked from his mind. I imagine his silent life here alive with inner dialogue, but I'll never know.

N'LILI SOME DOZEN YEARS AGO married my cousin Olivia. Olivia, my favorite cousin, took all of them unto her, in sickness and in health. Both my cousin and her partner are beautiful. N'Lili and I carry on an intense correspondence; she sends long handwritten letters, e-mails. She watches the moon—"we refer to that phase of the moon as the 'Cheshire' Moon, after the cat," they write—and like the moon her pronouns wax and wane. "I'm 'older' than your usual fan club but no less devoted," begins one letter to me, ending, "I can feel my own nightbirds coming out. 'The Girls' are night roamers. I'm getting younger. . . ." They e-mail over a cell phone and can only send or get a sentence at a time, in caps, like a ransom note. I write asking her about her birthday, and she answers that she celebrates both "beginning" and "emergence."

EMERGENCE IS WHEN I LEFT THE WOMB W/ THIS BODY.

AS N'LILI? I respond.

N'Lili writes, WE ARE WORKING VERY HARD TO LEARN NOT TO DIFFERENTIATE N'LILI & EVERYBODY. IT'S HARD THOUGH. NOT SURE I EVER WILL.

"It's like I feel a symphony inside me," she told me once.

N'Lili has Peggy and Annette, who collaborated on their name, and Rachel, and Naomi, and others. N'Lili is not female in body, but a man, barrel-chested, with strong broad calves and wide shoulders and tattoos up both arms. They tried dressing mostly as a woman but finally gave it up, though they still sometimes wear women's clothing or jewelry at home and do their nails always in sparkly polish.

"That [cross-dressing] lasted till I tried doing it in Amish country," she told me one day with a belly laugh, adding, "The fact is, I make an ugly woman."

At this point N'Lili has something like ten people left. I'm not sure exactly, nor are they ("All the kids R twins not related to each other. Some unknown to each other," she writes to me). The engine of the personalities is Peggy, an eight-year-old girl, "very vibrant," and, N'Lili tells me once, "out a lot around you." I talk to her a lot, though I also talk to Annie, Lily, Vicki, others, and sometimes "us," everybody together.

N'Lili, like many multiples, experienced abuse as a child, from a close male relative. "We are a contradiction internally as well as externally," she writes to me, in one of their handwritings, the tighter, more controlled one. "We are innocent and yet I have lived through horrors that are difficult for decent people to imagine."

AT CHRISTMAS THIS YEAR, I'm ailing. Olivia and N'Lili come over to visit and take turns curling up on the end of my bed. Olivia starts complaining about N'Lili in some way, just the random and meaningless complaints you make about the person you live with, if your cohabiting lasts more than a week.

"But that's okay," she says finally. "I could never settle for a one-head."

I lurk sometimes on message boards for folks with bipolar disorder. Lots of people talk about hearing voices. One woman posts that her manias cripple her with a drive for meaning. "It gets to the point where I can't go out with friends," she writes. "Everything has to mean something, be kind of a zen thing."

She got a lot of agreement, and it's worth pausing (though not too long) on the fact that the feeling that the world has meaning and should be shunned if it doesn't have meaning is a symptom of a classified disease. The clarity, or lack of clarity, of madness remains one of those questions about the mind that the mind itself may be unable to answer. How can we know what way of thinking is clearer or healthier, or if there really is a "type" or norm at all? It's like the question of depressive realism, a psychiatric belief in "the tendency of mildly depressed people to make accurate rather than self-serving biases, judgments, attributions and predictions," as a psychology text puts it. The accuracy of perception drives the illness—a Johnsonian perspective, arguing that no one is happy with what he is.

A Johns Hopkins psychologist wrote an article saying King Lear had bipolar disorder, beginning the play manic: the cocksure giveaway of his means, the demand for a spectacle of skyey praise from his daughters. Then, in a fit of manic fury, he banished Cordelia, descended into despair, and uttered his famous and much-quoted soliloquies on the nature of humans, "the poor forked animal," the ones who can be told and even believe they are "everything," but in the end are simply subject to rain, to wind, not ague-proof, open to water.

I can't, said the woman on the message board, just watch TV anymore.

AS WITH WORD AVERSIONS, I have always been sensitive to the sight of things, unusually so. I froze, during the trial, when the detectives talked about Kyle's use of detail and how it branded him as guilty. I see great swaths of things and find bizarre panoramas recorded in my notebook—*glaucous gulls fight while woman with bearskin nailed to the hood of her truck hauls furniture*—and tend to be hyperfocused, hyperdetailed. If they questioned me, those detectives, they would find me guilty. I would find myself guilty, though of what would be as strange as the threat posed by water.

When I remember my grandparents I remember mainly the aversion I felt—a primal horror really—to their faces, to the look of age, that difference that felt as if some larger hand had both scarred them and melted them. It's made me wonder lately how animals, the ones with visual acuity, like primates and birds, think of us. Because they see; my cat Savannah regards me for an hour from across the room; an orangutan I've worked with, Chantek, noticed a small scratch on a woman's hand from twenty feet away. Most mammals can get arthritis and cancer and a host of things. But there's nothing in the world of creatures like the taffy pull of gravity on the human face. Its razor marks of wrinkles; its knobs and bulbs and putty; its hobbles and humped luggage on the back. Under the eyes of the old, I keep noticing a mound that looks like a blank, sealed eye emerging through the skin, like death itself coming through. I saw Keats's death mask in Rome; his eyes looked just like that, like the pouches of age. I see it happening on my face, the plastic surgery of time. To forget our deaths as we do, the looming threat of meaninglessness, is an astonishing act of will.

Savannah sits and watches me, purring: poor, bare, forked animal, she might say.

RECENTLY MY FAMILY AND I drove ourselves to Newport, Oregon. Newport has, in its seaside strip, docks and docks of Steller's sea lions, so many you can hear their barking several miles away, all ages, indistinguishable, piled together. We stood on the piers, looking down on them in a reverie brought on by their rough rhythm, all but Jin, who thought he was going to fall down and be caught in the pile of cushiony bodies, the slamming flippers and bull necks.

I want to *go*, he whined.

Did you know they used to live on land? I told him to distract him. And if you opened those flippers, you'd find finger bones like your finger bones?

I saw this in a museum once: whalebones, the human hand hidden inside a flipper—so startling it felt like seeing my own body where it didn't belong.

Sometime millions of years ago the sea lions chose to climb back into the water, we told Jin (realizing *choice* was the wrong word; what's the right one for evolution? Slowly, slowly, they moved back out to the sea.)

They *chose* to? he said.

Then we stared down and who could tell who was looking at whom? The cacophony of the animals, their heads bent back almost double and black eyes fixed on the humans on the pier—babies in strollers, grandparents whose faces puffed, webbed, and fell—these mammals who had walked on the same ground we do, eaten greens presumably, and fowl, and meat. And if they'd stayed there maybe they would have begun to evolve toward depressive sea lions, Lear sea lions. Maybe they already have.

They're squawking at us like we're idiots, said Bruce, which was a joke, though it turned, as soon as it was uttered, into some kind of a primitive speculation—about us not knowing them, and them not knowing us, and how little we know.

Lear went to meet his daughter, Cordelia, at the edge of the sea.

Freud had a beautiful reading of *Lear,* in which Cordelia, saying only "nothing," represents Death, who in German folklore always appears as the mute character in the story. She doesn't keep
you in the grocery aisles showing you angels and eggplant, talking and talking. She stands with her head tipped, watching, in
front of the wine.

Lear tries to drive his Death away but at the end of the play
carries it by its wrung neck in his arms.

ONCE AT THE BEACH I yanked out my notebook and wrote
pretentiously of the ocean: *Like a mute tongue in a mute mouth. How
you wish you knew what it would say. How glad you are you don't know
what it would say.*

Stop, stop, my grandfather said, as if the water—that great
white weaving—would listen to him.

HEARING VOICES

A M I YOU, Mama?" my son Jin has asked me once or twice. It's a bathtub question. When Jin was small, not long speaking, he often asked things like that in the tub at night. I don't know why: deep, existential questions came to him as he sat cupped in the huge claw-foot tub like a dumpling in soup. Looking too like a little seal, long black hair slicked down.

"No," I said, "you're you," and he surveyed the bathroom doubtfully, seeing nothing to correspond to that.

Later, when he got used to being an *I*, he played pin-the-tail-on-the-donkey with that self. "No, *I* did that," he said about everything from buying our house to growing up in Macon, Georgia, where my husband grew up.

"I've lived out my life and now I'm a little guy again," he announced to me one day from the back of the car, old soul strapped into his harness. When Tommy Munsen died, Jin asked me if he had been the victim of that murder as well as the killer. His flesh unsettled, psyche soft as the Silly Putty he smears on newspaper pages, drawing up what picture it rubs against.

As he grows I watch his human consciousness settle on him like clothes that itch and fit, fit and itch, clothes being a good metaphor in that this consciousness we're not born wearing.

THERE'S AN OLD SPIRITUAL MALADY called "self-sickness." I have self-sickness. It makes me long to return to the dumpling stage. It makes me, too, want to survey the corners of the bathroom in confusion. What is it I'm sick of? My life, my thoughts, but what are those? Mine's a human life, existentially and skeletally like any other. I think. Or rather, *I think*. Thinking seems to be where all the trouble starts.

I am going to go down some of the time; I'm manic-depressive; it's built into my name. It's become common for the afflicted to append everything to themselves with *person with* or, perhaps, survivor: I am a person with epilepsy or Tourette's or cancer. Somehow I can't do that, imply this way of being glides by me like a ghost. Manic-depression is me.

But each pole of the bipoles functions almost as a distinct entity, so this morose one returns, my diploid cell, and I am introduced to her again. Oh, you. She drips a sour syrup from her mouth. I haven't met her in a while. She slumps around and reminds me of a lot of things I've almost forgotten: the time I tried to kill myself—the chalk of those tablets in my throat—the times I failed at something. She's not so much a talker as her counterpart, but she gets her points across and can be very factual and persuasive; she takes over, pushing at my eyes and at my stomach. We ridicule the other half of us for her confidence and her ambitions.

Of course that one will come sooner or later, telling her to put a sock in it. And I'll attend to her, too.

WE HAD A DINNER PARTY a few months ago and afterward, lying around being candid that way you do when you've both eaten and drunk too much, my friends and I started talking about how we thought. First my friend Rosina mentioned very idly— the way you do when you've eaten and drunk too much, even though in her case it's only ginger ale—about her daughter Beth leaving pieces of paper around the house scribbled with sequences of numbers. When she's alone, Beth said from her place in the corner, she imagines sequences of numbers and writes them down. When we asked Beth what kinds of sequences she saw, she tried to explain them to us but we couldn't understand her numerical chains, how they came to her. Then somehow we all started talking about things we do in our heads. Someone mentioned assigning colors to music. Bruce talked about a system of government he used to have up and running in his head all the time, with a president and elections and debates. If he failed to do enough writing or things went wrong in some way the government changed, so I guess it functioned more like the Italian government than the American one with its set terms. I used to feel vaguely guilty if we got into a big argument, because generally his government would take the blame for it and topple.

If you rule out a few transient depressions among my guests,

I was the only one present with a major psychiatric disorder. Perhaps there's no sense to the term *normal* after all.

AND YOU—the reader, that you. I wonder about your mind. In fact, if you were in front of me right now, I would ask you a million questions. Do you leave numbers scrawled on papers around the house or see musical notes as yellow? Do you find your mind irrelevant? And how in the world did we get to where we are, we humans?

Although if I met you, I might make you uncomfortable: I do ask a lot of questions; I pull at my hair and hold eye contact for too long and have odd mannerisms. I would want you to like me and open up to me. But perhaps it's easier this way.

It becomes a question to which I crave answers, perhaps to reassure myself of something, perhaps out of curiosity, one of the hallmarks of manic-depressives: Why do we think as we do? The question of how the basic, garden-variety neurotypical mind (if there is such a thing) developed is controversial, a subject of much study and much speculation that it's an unanswerable question: there's no angle from which the mind can peer into itself, as if I tried to diagnose a disease in my ear using my eyes. Who shapes them for you, those inner, conscious words that are your book, and reading *You are human* say *Yes I am* or *So what?* or *What foods do I need for dinner?* And see the end already, the chicken not just cut apart in plastic but mixed with olives and lemon, displayed, gnawed up.

I have a friend who reads the last five pages of any book first, then goes back to the beginning, reading toward it, a woman surfing on conclusion. She's Rosina, from my dinner party; her daughter litters the house with numbers. We like endings. We like points. Though *points* are the one thing history most surely strips away from us, if they're anything more complicated than mystery books or dinner. The flat earth with its stretched thread of horizon, A to B. Dante's ladderlike cosmos, runging from Satan's subfreezer to warmer Purgatory and hot Heaven.

Or the evolutionary Great Chain of Being, bacterial sludge and then a slightly humanoid primate and then the spinal cord straightening up like an arrow and then us. The point.

AUGUSTINE WROTE, *God, then, made man out of the dust of the earth.*

That would be a simple answer to the problem of how consciousness—and we—arose. But the fact is, Augustine, that God made man (as you put it) not once but many, many times.

God created man lithe and lumpy, man with the overhanging brow, plate-face man, man with a sagittal crest dividing his head to cement the strong muscles that helped him chew. This was man the vegetarian. Man the spear-tossing muncher of the boar haunch God also made.

Homo habilis, homo rudolfensis, the australopitheci, the ardipitheci. Homo floresiensis: hobbit man.

God's man lived in the jungles, he lived on the plains. He preferred bone and teeth for his tools, he preferred stone, he preferred wood. Half of him was woman.

Certain things inhered to most of God's men: they wore clothing, used tools, used fire. None had less than cunning. The human body reached its present, sprocket-hipped form 2 million years ago. As far back as 400,000 years ago he had hearth and hut. At least one hominid besides us—Neanderthal man, who also shared our brain size—folded its dead into graves, nurtured its weak, and played flute. Neanderthals may have spoken.

Nonetheless they're gone and we—Homo sapiens sapiens or Man Wise Wise—are left, the lone animal genus on the planet to have one species representative, one face, walking or crawling around. Hundreds of species of monkey and only one hominid, one human. Which gives Augustine the right to use the singular. Why us? Who knows? All the fossil record tells us is that our ancestors, Homo sapiens, wandered out of Africa about 100,000 years ago, and about 50,000 years ago developed the symbolic consciousness we know as fully human. Which means inner narration, voice: dictating to yourself what the chicken will become, and the world beyond the chicken. (As cognitive neuroscientist Merlin Donald says, "Fully human consciousness is inconceivable without language. Indeed, inconceivability itself is inconceivable without language.")

Scientists call this the Big Bang of the human mind.

After the Bang comes masterful and balletic and even senseless hunting. Art. Jewelry. Ritual. The images of horses and reindeer and bulls molder on the walls of caves. The art shows a mind not just reactive but reflective, able to plan. Modern humans, now called Homo sapiens sapiens, become an astonishingly dominant species. Many of the mammals they hunt, like the woolly mammoth, go extinct. Our kill sites show we sometimes kill far more than we can eat and just leave the carcasses on the ground (practicing? proving we can?), an unusual mammal behavior called "surplus killing."

In a museum once I saw the history of the world diagrammed upward, like a thermometer, with the space before the cosmic Big Bang labeled Time Before Time. We could call our early mental life Thought Before Thought.

AROUND THE TIME of our burst of consciousness, at least one other hominid vanished from the earth. We may have spelled doom for *Homo erectus,* and we probably meant the end of our kin the Neanderthal, who had thrived for over 100,000 years.

Smart, sociable, tender with their dead. In one case, fossil pollen tells us Neanderthals buried a corpse on a bed of spring flowers. Nonetheless a few millennia of us, and *pffft.* No more Neanderthals. We either proliferated wildly, driving them to the unsurvivable margins of their living space, or killed them off, we who are "tribal and aggressively territorial, intent on private space," writes Harvard biologist E. O. Wilson, of himself, and me, and you.

A group including a primatologist and a linguist created a prototype of Neanderthal language for the Discovery channel. It's simple and includes words like *oo-woo* for alarm and *mer* for anger.

What did the last group of, maybe, five Neanderthals—a family—say as the sleek, relatively denuded modern humans came ringing around their campfire? It is dark; they're on the edge of the pine-stepped Pyrenees. Nothing in the dark, like the saber-toothed cat lazily waiting, looks less foreign or more strange.

Oo-woo. Oo-woo. Mer.

I think we remember this early fratricide. I think we remember it as Cain and Abel, "the primal eldest curse," as Shakespeare wrote, "a brother's murder."

. . .

DOES ANYONE BELIEVE the story of the prodigal son as written? The elder son, who complained he worked and worked beside his father and had never been given so much as a kid to eat, was right: the prodigal's absence had nothing to do with that perverse outflow of affection. Who knows why the older wasn't the fatted-calf child? Clearly the younger—the one of the "riotous living"—had charm, had life, maybe from an early age pulled funny clothes over his head and ran across the house, making everyone laugh. Maybe the older got plain and serious.

How did God watch the hominids, like sons, work out their inheritance? Neanderthals had more body hair, thicker bodies; they should have survived the ice ages, not us. Maybe God felt the wrong child lived. Or maybe we're the undeserving favored ones, sitting down to eat the banquet we scarcely appreciate, always amoral and amusing.

Who always get one hundred fancy things for each thing we ask for, ninety-nine things too much.

I say this as an environmental abnormality, a craps roll of Darwin's dice, a destructive, carnivorous primate, myself.

AND YOU? You have not killed anyone. You have sat in a chair, reading, alive in the present of your body and the earth and the gasses you breathe: and also in the book of your head. As anthropologist Ian Tattersall says, "While every other organism we know about lives in the world as presented to them by Nature, human beings live in a world that they consciously symbolize and re-create in their own minds. Which is what makes us such fascinating—and dangerous—creatures."

But you are not dangerous. You are the kind of person who reads books.

In fact, you are more likely than anything to be like me: anxious—which 25 percent of people have been, clinically, needing treatment—and depressed, which 10 percent of the U.S. is in any given year, or plagued by other irritations born of those neuronal connections that helped scalp the planet millennia ago. Your place in the biological order isn't likely to have puffed up your ego; rather, consciousness has probably turned its honed Paleolithic sharpnesses to you. Though, as a member of a species, it defines you, knighting you with your second *sapiens;* without it, you would be a premodern human, an oaf. Not the man Augustine talks about at all.

WILLIAM CALVIN'S THEORY about our minds, which he details in his book *A Brain for All Seasons,* argues that the neuronal connections needed for us to become conscious and linguistic developed as the climate changed and humans began to hunt for grazing animals in coordinated bands. It's easy to see how it would take a good deal of mental apparatus, including the consciousness to form complex utterance, to surround and bring down an auroch, ancestor of the cow. And presumably we find ourselves sooner or later with humans who have to ask whether we should be or not be, whether 'tis nobler, and others for whom it becomes impossible to face life without a squeeze machine, like autistic Temple Grandin. Because we have done a poor job of weeding ourselves down, or because the universe loves diversity, or because humanity, having occupied virtually every niche on the planet, now needs to itself become more complex. Or just because.

THERE ARE, I've discovered, doctors researching the role of mental illness in human evolution—not doctors who investigate how to eradicate it but doctors who look at how mental illnesses have contributed to human evolution and the flourishing of our species. One way of looking at this centers around memes, or mental concepts—"the genes of culture," as Richard Dawkins puts it in *The Selfish Gene*. Different minds create new memes, as necessary for the freshening of culture as new genetic combinations are vital to the freshening of the species. Bipolars—"restless and unquiet," as one correspondent puts it—may have helped with the spread of human culture, migrating frequently and often into new territories. The doctor who tells me this, Antonio Preti of the University of Cagliari in Italy, a founder of the Schizophrenia Project, which studies the disease both in the aspects of its treatment and its creativity, writes me:

> Evolution, i.e., our chance to adapt to new and unprecedented environments depends on genetic variability. In this respect, there are no defective people: simply, someone hosts genes that imply a higher risk of mood instability, and this might be linked to adaptive potentials for the individuals or the group to which he/she belongs. We cannot foresee when, and how, these peculiar characteristics of these

individuals will save our species, at the price of their own damnation, sometimes.

AT MY DINNER PARTY my friend Penny stretches her neck back and laughs, though we don't know why. She crooks a long leg out.

She is saying, I never feel guilty, ever.

I tell her, I always feel guilty.

I do. I have been known to drive around the block, shaking, if a police car's parked anywhere near my house. I have to talk to myself about the fact that they're not there to arrest me, though I'm forty-eight years old and boring, and don't even jaywalk much anymore.

Penny says, I can't imagine that at all.

Preti writes to me, "By the way, since bipolar disorders have a conservative rate of 1–2% in the general population, well beyond the awaited spontaneous mutation rate (0.01%), in the past something happened to maintain the bipolar disorders genes, whatever they are, in the general pool."

MY ST. AUGUSTINE'S *CONFESSIONS* was translated by a man named Pine-Coffin, a name I didn't notice for years on the flyleaf of my flaking Penguin edition, but one that, once I noticed it, I realized couldn't be anybody other than Augustine himself, in disguise. Who else would remind us so naggingly of our mortality, both inside and outside the book?

I noticed the name right when Augustine wanted me to, at an Augustinian moment in my life—middle-aged, feeling that sad creature visiting again, and suddenly full of dread at the things around me, harmless before as grass. Could it be time, again, to stand under a hosing of water, pull fabrics around my spreading form, drive somewhere, to stand in a classroom and say things I've said so many times they've lost any meaning for me? To eat? To pack clothes soiled with the fluids of plants and animals into the washing machine, pour in soap, turn the dial? Again? When did this againness fall so hard? It is the biblical plague of locusts, the rain of terrible small things.

In the mornings my knees shake, and my lips.

It's maybe more persuasive even than Augustine's book (persuasive as that is) that he would make this move: be two people at once, one ancient and one modern, to demonstrate that principle of all times being contained in the present, and to show his disdain even for his own words, by slapping them into the poorly fitting clothes of another tongue. He was a sly one, that Augustine, a reason to add even a third *sapiens* after *Homo,* and it's impossible to imagine the Neanderthal, with his fuddled brow, doing these kinds of dances with language.

THIS PLACE IS A SHAMBLES, I take to saying, or, My life is a shambles, calling my home or my life by an archaic word meaning a blood-spattered butchershop, via an older word for *table,* borrowed to mean the tables that once displayed fresh-killed meat.

One night in my sleep I turn over and my love hears me say, *I live on the rue Disaster.*

I won't live on the *rue,* that crooked street, forever. My own prodigal, Manic Girl, will come back. She will talk far too much, with that manic pressure of speech—the words sluiced out, not quite coherent—spend too much, overcommit herself. She will dance wildly in the fields, reject what binds her, and wait for the fatted calf to be slain.

I feel like someone carved me out like a pumpkin, I wrote as a young girl. She, like me, would have no idea who Manic Girl is.

MAYBE THE REASON N'Lili and I love each other lies in the fact that we each have so many secrets from ourselves, not ones constructed by walls of avoidance but ones constructed by the architecture of ourselves. I know what Manic Girl does, but when I'm not her I find her quite extraordinary, as she does me. She aims lipstick at her mouth and finds herself rather fetching. I halt at my own ugliness, rubbery scarring and lithium acne's corrosion.

I do not write books for publication. I would never dare. She does.

N'Lili's challenge in his life, as a "many-head," has been to let the women that are him work together. I aim at this as well.

"Look," I can say to Bruce, "talk to me about this when I'm a little manic, okay?"

IN ORDER for some of us to become so alienated from ourselves, we need a tool with which to construct those selves. In our

Big Bang of consciousness, we began to narrate the world to ourselves: to hear voices in our head. At first, I imagine, we had
scarcely a few words, just enough to contribute to survival, then
gradually the neuronal connections began to build and the inner
narrative became more frivolous—not just *antelope over there* but
I look good peering into a pond. At some point this simple linguistic
coordinating consciousness made way for the circus a person like
me carries in her head.

Inner narrative, even at its most neurotypical, forms an inaccu-
rate voice. Light proceeds into our eyes, and our brains manufacture color. Who knows if my red is your red? Students in a Harvard
study, told to watch teams passing a basketball, half the time missed
a man in a gorilla suit walking into the room and standing amid the
ball passers. Studies of memory uncover even more falsehood—bits
of films you've seen, implants from stories you've heard.

In a sense, then, we could call our inner world a kind of insanity. If my voices begin to say *the world would be better off without
you,* that's less surprising than the fact that such voices exist at all;
the thought may perhaps be justified, while its ability to be present in such form must astonish.

And you, reader? Do you hear praise or blame, tasks or satisfaction? *My cat is hungry; my daughter Sylvia is not the girl I wanted.*

If consciousness is narrative, largely fictional narrative, somewhere back we stepped over the line into fantasy creatures. You,
living in your head, might as well be a unicorn. Writing books—
piling new narratives onto each one's internal mythical narrative—
is a kind of surplus killing.

Mine becomes a bodily sadness, the sour syrup dripping: my
tongue gets a tongue-sadness, my lungs, my liver. My voice slows

down, like the whales'. I say things like *Why get up? Why pick up my things off the floor?*

I'm talking to Jim Nollman one day, my whale-music friend, about the things we've used to distinguish ourselves from animals in the past. Mostly we've lost these distinctions, as they surface in animal groups: tool use, cultural grouping, language. What's left? Suicide?

"Suicide," he echoes. "I guess that's about it."

MY AUNT WRITES ME THAT, in a book, I've turned a poor depressed man into a monster. I wrote about my grandfather, her father. And I guess I have turned him into a monster, using what stuck up in the silt of memory, disregarding how my life extends onto the lives of others, its small place in the cacophony of human narratives. I did not explore the possibility that I'm a monster, too, which of course I am. It's what we have to distinguish us, *Homo suicidalus,* poor depressed monsters all.

EDWARD O. WILSON, Harvard biologist, writes: "Perhaps a law of evolution is that intelligence [in a species] usually extinguishes itself."

YOU'RE ALWAYS SABOTAGING YOURSELF, my husband Bruce tells me. Whenever something good happens to you, you turn it into something terrible. It's *classic* depressive behavior.

Did I mention how I love him? Aficionado of breath, I find his choice, wild grass with a bit of cedar. Do other people find it as wonderful as I do simply to smell the ones you love? I have a habit of getting inches away from his mouth to have a conversation, just to enjoy his breathing. I know him this way: I am a good animal. He's right about all he tells me. He says it because he loves me, and favors me feeling good.

We have this conversation so much we could be having it anywhere, at our cheap scratched dining table with its burned-down candles—gargoyles of drip—in Carnival glass.

What if it's useful to sabotage myself? I ask him. Maybe everybody should be depressed. Most people are pretty happy, and half the species in the world are dying.

I tell him, No rainforest, no ozone.

He knows all this of course.

He will be digging his nails into the candledrip, mounding the gargoyles, pinching and sculpting. You don't have to feel bad about everything.

I tell him yes, as a moral principle, beyond a biochemical one, as a dignified response to my species legacy, I've decided I ought to feel bad about everything. A grandiose and pointless gesture, in line with my human heritage.

HAMLET, who wouldn't cast his nighted color off, embodies melancholy. Dr. Brigham writes that he had Hamlets in his asylum, no doubt annoying, after a while, with their questions. We do not tolerate perseverating questions in adults, who ought to know by now what kind of a piece of work is man. But depression brings the need to ask, with the taste of blood in your mouth,

why you and your kind exist at all, how we can be both the quin-
tessence of dust and yet delight not.

It makes me need to understand the whole accident or design,
however you want to call it, of evolution. I don't think it's possible to know why human beings exist, why Neanderthals don't
still mark the earth with their heavy footprints and flung flowers,
why we survived at all, as we almost didn't. Why have a creature
that comes to exist only to ask why it should exist, and on top of
that, pays money to go to theaters and hear itself ask why it stays
alive? Finding that question perhaps the most effective theater of
all. Our love of *Hamlet,* given the number of species we've wiped
out, feels almost rude. I find myself, this visitor with the bloody
lips, bizarre. And I'm finding everyone around me not just unde-
lightful, as Hamlet did, but bizarre as well.

WHAT KIND of a piece of work is man? If you stumbled onto a
Neanderthal or a Homo s. sapiens living site, you would have a
hard time distinguishing them at first—you would find the same
fire pit, dents maybe where a skin roof clung to the ground. If you
could compare the two, you would notice the s. sapiens site already demonstrating a sense of order: a spot for piling wood, a
spot for hacking out axes, a spot for sleep. We are a compulsive
people. There is a place in our world just for reindeer bones, for
tusks, for fire. As opposed to Neanderthals, who didn't care how
their things mingled.

And you would sense everywhere in our world the double
life of symbol, with animals painted on the walls of caves, carved
big-bellied women, our dead buried with vests of mammoth-tusk

beads, spears, and axes in their arms—a richer bounty to speed the way through the afterlife than we probably ever gave our living.

We could *see* death in our heads, a place, a time, a theater of killing, self-defense, and wealth. And since these spear throwers could presumably kill or be killed—else why have weapons at all?—our death itself contained death. And opened onto a whole other world of death, a free fall through spaces of place and time.

Once consciousness swallows the world, it cannot imagine gorging it up again.

(And we find our dead so remote—rude even!—in their abandonment of our society. My son takes by the hand a friend named Summer, leading her to a dead robin, a bird we found the day before with a bloody smear across its lower body: vivid replica of its breast. At the time Jin felt the need to bury the bird under a pile of grass clippings, dropped leaves, and mauve rhododendron petals. Now he disentombs it with a sweep of the foot.

"It's dead, Summer," he tells her. "Being dead is very serious and very, very complicated.")

I am wandering through my house, one Homo sapiens sapiens, doubly wise, so wise my wisdom demands twice utterance. Without thinking very much, I cram my arms full of things and, at various stations around the place drop them, like a sorting robot: the Buzz Lightyear squawking about Star Command goes into the toy chest, coffee cups go in the sink, socks get underhanded to the hamper. I have a room for sleeping, a room with a space for eating and for the beehive of a rolltop desk, a room just for sitting in front of the black lozenge of my laptop. I have a room for washing my body and voiding its used solids and liquids and, lately, for pulling white hairs from my head with tweezers, a tool that's been around for several thousand years. The white hairs all grow from one patch of skull, and their wiry texture's unlike anything I've ever grown from my head, as if some other woman, a coarse lop-browed Neanderthal woman, is pushing out there. No matter how many I remove, hundreds stay. I patiently, painfully, yank the evidence of her. I wouldn't do this in any other room.

I have paintings on the walls, and a stove at one end of my living room, not particularly exciting facts, but interesting in that our 50,000-year-ago humans would feel at home with my choices, and not just the practical choice of heat. Art bloomed on their walls. We favor portraiture, though, and in the Paleolithic, human figures rarely show up. Mostly it's a pour of enormous mammals, all capable of killing: aurochs with enormous horns; bulky prehistoric horses; hairy rhinoceroses; reindeer; bison; panther. In one human image at the Shaft of the Dead Man, in Lascaux, a prone man lies under a bison, apparently dead. He's done in white, a simple outline like a police figure, unlike the rich reds and blacks of the other mammals, painted in ocher and charcoal and other tints mixed with animal fat. The creatures cascade along the walls, hooves or paws flared at the midlevel of their bulk, not as if they're jumping or falling but as if they've never known gravity. Manes stream in the rock-wind.

Our cosmos preyed on us and we knew it. While we preyed, too, it could reverse the process at any time. We lived like drug dealers or crime lords, whose riches are bought at the price of a hundred assassins drifting through each day's darkness. And we loved or at least admired what deaths posed themselves, getting right every wrinkle on the rhinoceros, its small melancholy eye, as opposed to our blank image of ourselves. A French scientist believes we achieved our work's misty pointillist look by spit painting—chewing the pigment and spitting the paint from our mouths, using the lip and tongue control developed by our new speech.

Those painters, in the Big Bang of the mind, developed the ability to spit the fully imaginary—an artist painted a unicorn at Lascaux, its one horn spearing up the cave wall. There are abstract paintings composed of patterns of scarlet dots, and other symbols, like a charcoal cross in the Brunel Chamber of Chauvet.

Wiping out the Neanderthals must have been a largish lesson: we could be the ocher bison with its horns, not the white outline. We could take something the cosmos had handed to us— something that inconveniently got in our way at times—and simply erase it from the world. We became E. O. Wilson's "exterminator species," and the species that would have the mind to know itself as that. And we became the artists who must have stood in a creative trance at Lascaux, pulling from the storage of their brains memories that became the curved lofting creatures so eerily lovely you look at them. And look. And don't care what else their creators did.

Humans living earlier in time—the australopithecines, the pithecanthropi—scavenged their meat meals. They found bodies and dug the marrow out of the bones, a needed source of protein: harmless as a crow pecking at roadkill. Neanderthals scavenged a great deal, and when they killed, they got close and they suffered. Homo sapiens sapiens brought art to hunting, with a choreographed killing style and a proliferation of projectile weapons:

spears, javelins, the spear thrower called the atlatl. As we began to eat meat 2 million years ago our brains began growing, and as climate change and drought forced us to live off grazing animals 50,000 years ago, symbolic consciousness followed that more complicated diet. We needed to plan, to speak in order to coordinate our movements, not just pick berries and dig roots.

William Calvin details the burst of human language out of hunting, the hungry need for conceptualization, the fact that the language area of the brain and the throwing area are almost identical.

And psychosis may be in there as well, a "hitchhiker allele," as Preti says, attached to the part of consciousness governing linguistic skill.

These thoughts, any thoughts, shape themselves in an arena growing out of a complicated and worshipful relationship with death. To excel, in this universe of stab and stagger. Certainly language fueled our social sense, our creation of human hierarchies. From the evidence of our burial sites, some of us had far more things, went to our graves with a great deal more fanfare, than others; certainly we lived in tiers of importance as well. And we accelerated, with language, our development of killing tools: toggle-headed harpoons, spear throwers, finally the bow and arrow.

If language is a killing tool, handed down to us from the first small grunt-coordinated javelin thrusts, it bears this mark: the reek of blood, the coarse hairs from the downed bull that must have marched like a demigod through the world before those grunts came to *mean:* throw. Language thrusts and flenses not just in a political sense but a personal one as well. Your inner narrative will at times attack you as mine does me.

· · · ·

WHAT ARE WE TO SAY for ourselves, the survivors' survivors? The chatterboxes? Whose world cannot live with us, while we often cannot live with ourselves. I see a ginkgo tree outside my window; its unevolved fronds could have fed a dinosaur. And the ferns, which could have been nibbled on by an apatosaurus, or a prehistoric reindeer, as happily as they can now be consumed by the overmultiplying deer, who lack their natural predators, the cougars, the wolves. The fish in my bay negotiate their world with the primitive brains that still nestle in our own skulls, under the complicated hominid modifications of looping cortex. We—myself, and you, reader, whom literary tradition would term *gentle*—were parented by those who squirmed their way through eons of evolution, changing, moving around, driving to extinction, one way or another, those who most resembled them, and those whose bodies fed their bodies and their art.

Early modern humans sometimes buried their dead on their sides, knees tucked up to elbows and head on the hands, in the posture of Rodin's *The Thinker*.

I HAVE all over the house—on the desk where I write, with its peeling overly perfect fake-wood surface—dinosaur stickers Jin's been leaving everywhere. He also has early mammals: mastodon, woolly mammoth. Again we find these prey of ours fascinating, as did the painters in the dim caves in the Pyrenees. A French scientist is trying to clone woolly mammoths, using DNA taken from a well-preserved mammoth carcass in Siberia. Jin may share the planet with them again, a luxury no human child has had for ten millennia.

We took Jin to see a mammoth reconstructed in a science museum; it was surrounded by wax human hunters, who each wore a spear of some sort and a snarl. This, too, is a false premise, I think; they would have looked like painters or dancers, focused, a little on edge, but generally secure in their mastery.

Writer Robert Hass says we have technes or skills of life and technes of death: poetry versus the bomb. I wonder if the two can be teased apart.

AUGUSTINE SAID, *Perhaps we are what You want to remember.*

Then again, I like to think about what consciousness was before early modern man, the humans we think we understand—they are so like us, with their sorting and their murdering and their art. Some theorists of the mind, like Merlin Donald, believe consciousness switched on like a lightbulb in that tempestuous age 50,000 years ago, that the neurons and cerebral columns suddenly began working together to emit these spasms of thought. Before then, humans existed in a way that was reactive and unmediated by self-conscious awareness.

If you believe in such an emergence, consciousness arose out of a simple piling up of neurons. As brain capacity grew—a naturally selected advantage—the neurons sparked out of their purpose of more accurate but thoughtless reactions and became something else altogether: something sluggish by comparison, maybe, but powerful in the way of all things large and smothering: Concepts. Names.

Ian Tattersall points out the mistake of believing evolution means an accretion of desirable qualities. Creatures that survive move their genes forward, the whole package—negatives, neutrals too—as long as the whole continues. There's lots of evolutionary flotsam in there: the appendix, the gill slits in embryos, even body hair. See yourself as a Frankenstein being, stitched together from a geologic graveyard of parts. So it may be with the mind: love, guilt, consciousness itself could be accidents, a common belief in consciousness studies. Side effects, something our too-efficient bodies drag along—what scientist Julian Huxley calls "the accidental emergence of purpose in the universe through the evolution of human consciousness."

The accidental emergence of purpose.

So there were moments, somewhat like those early birds idly flapping their stubs, when consciousness began and flicked off. Trying itself out.

I picture, in that moment, a woman. She would have looked surprisingly familiar to you, I think—the cave clothes not too different from some outfits of the 1960s, though she'd have a shag of hair, worn teeth. She gnawed on the fresh marrow of a reindeer, when suddenly she saw herself, a woman gnawing on a bone. The food was what she craved, that's true (delicious), but still she saw herself, unnerving—why should she be there at all, a woman chewing marrow?

A woman whose tucked form, let's say, will be cast forever at the base of a cave somewhere. She will never *see* herself, not as the men who carefully brush dirt off the imprint of her skeleton will see her. But, for a minute, an image may rise to her out of a pool of water in her memory. She puts that image together with this self she catches appearing in front of her like a picture, chewing out black, hidden meat. It's the mask she feels suddenly, fitting loosely over this consciousness of hers. Terrifying, maybe, for the seconds it lasts—the senseless way the universe coalesces in a point behind her eyes.

Then she gets thirsty or something, and it's done.

I can call her Eve, the mother of thought. Her awareness has seeded mine, an awareness that as long as I can remember has periodically visited the question of destroying itself, along with the question of buying Frosted Cocoa Mocha to smear on my lips, wearing my paper dress, or cleaning my house. The doctors I see assure me I shouldn't take my own frequent animus toward myself personally. Their evidence being that it's fixable: and it's true, I haven't really felt this way in a long time. Though it would seem evolution, which has handled the opposable thumb and so forth with such aplomb, could have stopped a portion of the population from wanting to rip its own skin off. One answer is that evolution doesn't solve everything (which is true). Another is that we Hamlets serve a purpose.

I HAD THAT EVE FEELING at seven years old, heading down the street to Sid's candy store. I wasn't quite there yet; I could see the tiny candy store, the littery corner, while I could also see in anticipation my favorite things inside, the box of giant red wax lips, the packages of fleshy pink bubble gum—Bazooka, my favorite. I thought of these treats and their sugary, nonfood flavors and I thought of other things on the other tracks of my mind, like what you'd find if you flew to the end of space and why cats had to die before people and many other subjects—I did that at that age—when suddenly my brain took a deep, deep stagger. Why was there a room in my head to put all these things, anyway? Why did the world keep plummeting into me, and what was *me?*

I had a picture of myself as the infinitesimal point of ink at the tip of an enormous V that was the entire universe, as if I were (this simile wouldn't have existed for me at the time) the black hole into which everything collapsed. I was too young to know that everyone around me on the street—my father, irritable in his butter-colored Bermuda shorts, young moms in red talons and floral prints—was a black hole, too.

The hell'd you drag me here for if there's nothing you want? said my dad, when I stood stupidly in the store. He was not one to brook fools—or existential nausea—gladly. I remember wanting to want something in the old, uncomplicated way, the tongue-and-lips way, a drive for the simple, sweet plush of pleasure.

To have consciousness is to have the illusion at least that the world has chosen you to be its vessel, its mixing bowl. Though I learned in reading consciousness theorist Daniel Dennett that about a third of the population has just this experience at about this age. And perhaps for many of us it's the last experience of consciousness as singular, as pure, that is to come.

AMONG THE BEAUTIFUL CROWS

I CAN REMEMBER, sometime in the last few years, skulking around: I never stopped in front of a window. Someone out there wanted to shoot me in the back. Even now, as an absurd memory, it seems other than a thought. My skin winced in front of the window: the bullet seemed to have parted the air already. Though a little before that time everything had been magnificently possible, my own life symphonic. Not in belief only but in a deep intestinal relish. Manic Girl had arrived. If I imagined something, it would happen. I couldn't watch a motorcycle whish down my street; if I thought of it crashing, it would crash. These are normal, treatable, moments, and the memory itself does not interest me. What I'm groping toward are the bits that linger afterward. My skin parting and vulnerable, the image of the downed motorcycle, the sense of the rent in the world left by tragedy.

My cat giving me messages when I was a child, and the crows

whose language I've taught myself as an adult, and can speak roughly: *Caw caw caaaaw,* I say, spreading scraps. *Safe food.* I love the crows, and fault my goofily loving outdoor cat, Friend, only for sometimes scaring them away. My crows drop shellfish from the harbor and horse chestnuts onto the asphalt of my street, aiming for the tire tracks, sometimes kicking their version of canned food into the paths of cars, who helpfully crack it open.

I'm reading an article titled "Creativity, Evolution and Mental Illnesses" by Antonio Preti, the psychiatrist I mentioned earlier, and Paola Miotto. I just finished an old article written by Nancy Andreasen, a professor of psychiatry at the University of Iowa, who studied the Iowa Writers' Workshop and found approximately one-third of the students mood-disordered, many of them bipolar.

"Without social confrontation new memes cannot become diffuse," write Preti and Miotto. "Studies on the link between creativity and mental illnesses show that it is exactly the characteristics of the mental disorder which also confer some advantage on afflicted individuals. These advantages extend to the groups to which the creative, mentally ill individuals belong." The authors cite bipolar disorder for its "greater sensitivity and acuteness," and value other qualities of mental disorders, such as enhanced associational thinking and fewer gating mechanisms for outside stimuli, allowing a torrent of information to pour in—difficult for the mind to manage, but leading toward new conceptualizations and more inclusive thinking.

Mental disorders, these authors argue, have always played and continue to play a key role in evolution. Perhaps they are the secret advantage we have over intelligent machines.

The technology—genetic engineering, genetic selection—is close to being in our grasp to eliminate my kind; we are not yet seen as part of the group's "adaptive advantage," to quote Preti and Miotto again. Freeman Dyson's probably right; parents won't knowingly allow their children to have conditions like mine.

A CORRESPONDENT of mine named Suz—who has Asperger's and manages a large Asperger's website—thinks neurodiversity ultimately describes everyone: like ethnic diversity, she writes. I tend to believe this, too: it describes the human range. For all of us, consciousness is a spectacularly private and particular phenomenon. Though as with ethnicity there will always be those on the marginalized ends of the spectrum, who make others uncomfortable, whose lifeways—whose mind ways—pose a challenge when they're seen and they're heard.

Emily Dickinson wrote to her often befuddled mentor, Thomas Higginson, "All men say 'What' to me but I thought it a fashion."

What? say my students to me when I talk to them about Emily Dickinson.

What? they say, a lot.

Suz writes to me, when I ask her what she wants her website to accomplish:

> When I say neurodiversity I mean like ethnic diversity. . . . By looking upon neurodiversity as a positive thing . . . maybe when it comes to it people will make better decisions about what types of genetic engineering they will do than they otherwise might have done.

. . .

ODDLY ENOUGH, as we become more and more obsessed with the feature we consider our defining one, consciousness (and for consciousness to survey itself is rather awful; no one could stand to watch a television that delivered a running critique of itself, yet we're forced to contain one), and as consciousness studies grows into a real field, those who study consciousness find it less and less real. Real both philosophically and literally, as an agent in the world. In the mid-1980s, neurophysiologist Benjamin Libet set up an experiment to try to measure the lag time between the will to act and the start of action. Volunteers marked on a precise oscilloscopic clock the time when they chose to flex a finger, while electrodes monitored the low-level brain activity needed to begin movement. The low-level, unconscious brain activity came about half a second before the decision to act, which almost immediately preceded movement. Parsing out the time, Libet found each person spent about ten times longer unconsciously getting ready to move than he or she did thinking and then moving. Libet concluded consciousness has little active role in our lives except perhaps the ability to veto an act. At most, wrote a Libet follower, we have no free will, just "free won't."

Work like Libet's has led to theorizing that consciousness has no real agency in our lives, except in choosing a way to narrate accomplished events to itself. We act on involuntary impulses coming from the brain and nervous system; we convert the acts into stories—of guilt, redemption, love, and reason.

The *I* of consciousness, the twig from which we date ourselves as modern humans, has no point. It's the ultimate bureaucrat. From here to there it just shoves messages across the desk.

Part of me resists the thought that consciousness means nothing, just when those whose neurons are wired differently begin to find a voice for ourselves, to say who we are and how we wish to be regarded. I suppose a neurologist would point out to me the difference between volition and perception, controlling what you do versus how you experience what you do.

ROBERT HASS, whose comments about technes of life and technes of death have stuck with me, told me to remember that one of the first human artistic forms was tragedy. I don't know him; I asked him to talk to me and he did, at a small cafe with lukewarm coffee and a front on the cold Pacific; it was, as we sat comfortably filled with warm liquid, the day of Thomas Munsen's murder, though of course we didn't know that. Thomas was probably "pestering" Kyle Anderson, asking Kyle about the tubes and filters in his pond, even as we idly talked tragedy.

"The point of tragedy is, What's it like when you really fuck up?" said Hass. "Everything's utterly destroyed and it's one of the first things we ever thought about." Is tragedy a techne of life or of death? I don't know. Thanks to a MacArthur Fellowship, Bob, as he calls himself, is a certified genius, under the California denim and hiker's good looks, and his mind wanders to tragedy, which you could define as the awakening of the mind to its own acts. "What's it like when you really fuck up?"

It's like this: the gods spin you into it, viewers pity you, and you talk about it endlessly.

. . .

THAT WOULD MAKE CONSCIOUSNESS a kind of torture.

I don't say this. Bruce says this. We're walking on rocks at the edge of the Puget Sound, looking for starfish in tide pools. Jin's there, too, and our friend Brenda; we take turns holding Jin's arms to pull him over the boulders. It's the kind of rock that's cooled lava, with bubbles crusted into stone, very sharp; our nerves narrate this fact to our consciousness; even through sneakers it scrapes the tender bottoms of our feet. Above the rock-and-pebble beach there's a spotty layer of madrona trees, doing their astonishing move of growing straight out and then up, as if they're divided by their loyalties to water and sky; then the towering Sitka spruce. Mallards, an occasional muscular flash of swimming seal. All these things, in the best of human wisdom, do not narrate this day to themselves: not as we do, gathered around a tide pool admiring a purple starfish, which has one arm canted to an L, the rest straight against the rock. We all touch him, which he gives no sign of minding: he's hard as a shoe, covered with tough pimples the same unnatural purple color, the shade of Barney the dinosaur.

Did you know starfish have no brains, only mouths that go straight to a stomach? says Bruce. A mouth and a stomach—that's how they exist.

We've been talking about the half-second delay, the lives we live beyond volition. This thought gives me a new way, both justified and despairing, of thinking about my own life. What's made this mess? This shambles? Something buried under the folds of what I think of as *me*.

Brenda murmurs something about Buddhist no-mind, balanced like a child's wobble toy on the rocks. Here at the literal littoral.

This is what we're thinking, to explain why our bodies and neurons have directed us here. As we touch the hermit crabs, they slide away; the anemones draw dreadlocks around our fingers; but the starfish, that thing so different in color from the grayed greens and whites around it that it seems man-made, couldn't care less. Its stomach thinks nothing. Its stomach doesn't think.

Brenda and I have been talking about how we might reincarnate as one of these, consequence of a pointless life: or evolve from a simple piece of sea life to the complex human intelligence we are, able to achieve Buddhahood.

Maybe it's the other way around, says Bruce. Maybe we're made to evolve backward, so we go from full consciousness to less and less to none. Maybe we want to be starfish in the end.

We look for a while longer at the starfish, motionless under the rustling olive-green water, though Jin lightly tugs at its arms every once in a while. It is fearless, undissuadable. Mouth and stomach: never a taste but the flavor of pure existence.

I THINK OBSESSIVELY about volition after that, about the small hand stirring the starfish water, his brilliantly innovative opposable thumb couching a crescent of dirt. His hair thick and straight, inclining to muss, large eyes with an epicanthic fold, dimples, and skin a shade more olive than mine, though mine's quite olive. His face resets my standard of beauty.

Of the babies I lost through miscarriage I think: I could never have loved those children the way I love this child. The smell of his breath, his skin, his thumbs with their lunar dirt, the rushed, jailed creature of his heart. His humor, his deep belly laugh. The kisses, still almost mammal lickings.

In the mornings he will not get out of bed. Instead he wakes up and chants, "Mama Mama Mama," a vesper. When he hears my footstep on the stairs he calls out, "Mama?" like he's afraid that sometime in this day-in-and-day-out routine I will be someone else. When I answer him, he calls out, "Mama! I love you!" in relief. I carry him to my bed for cartoons.

I AM, I guess, a Comings success story, having failed to breed from my body. Or a Comings demo model, showing the kind of neurasthenic creature our great Homo sapiens sapiens line has come to.

What does this kind of selection look like over a few millennia? Let's open (as Peter Ward does in his book *Future Evolution,* when he refers to "These children that in another age would die early, but here will live and even breed") the possibility that Comings is right. What would it be, Comings's "grotesque form of species-specific genetic meltdown"? The rate of selection of undesirable genes, he writes, threatens to "destroy the species from within," after creating a world wracked with anxiety, suicide, jails full of those who can't control themselves. Comings suggests genetic testing of all pregnancies, with offers of termination for reasons ranging from genes for violent behavior to genes for obesity.

If we don't act, Comings writes, the species will "become a genetically different one than it used to be."

And no one wants that new jewel on the evolutionary chain.

. . .

MY HUSBAND BRUCE'S PARENTS drank themselves to death by the age of fifty—his father had received a quick psychiatric discharge from the Marines before going anywhere, and behaved like a bipolar. Bruce has none of these chromosomally flawed qualities except a real, but somewhat comical, love of gambling. Though he only gambles two or three times a year, playing craps, he does it with a bug-eyed, shiny-skinned thrill that shows dopamine high-beaming. Other than these craps binges he's a poet, and a man with a genius IQ who loves particle physics.

Most refutations of Comings say these disorders aren't increasing or that increases come from other factors—the growing stress of a technological age, or simply the pour of toxins in our environment. Autism clusters have sprung up around particularly toxic areas, like Brick Township, New Jersey. For whatever reason, clinicians I know agree, anecdotally, that emotional and behavioral disorders are on the rise. Some, like autism, are showing documented increases. I suspect if you polled mental health workers you'd get a lot of agreement with Comings's theory of the gene bomb. (A nurse said to me about my boy, "You're lucky you got a good one. My niece adopted a boy who's causing all kinds of trouble now. Bad genes." "The genes weren't there," my neighbor says, of Kyle Anderson, adding that "the genes weren't there" in the victim, either. My genes, certainly, are somewhere, but not *there*. Genes seem to exist like draft numbers in the 1960s, intractably on your side and saving you from guerrilla warfare, or not.)

I always wonder, What if a theory's right, but it's all for different reasons? What if we need to breed another kind of human, and the so-called undesirables breed because what they offer moves toward what's necessary or desirable? Maybe sadness is the new medicine.

Think of autistic Temple Grandin, distanced from language, designing her revolutionary humane slaughterhouse. Into her machines half of America's cattle—rebred descendants of the aurochs—go to die, with peace at least in their predation. I imagine slaughtering cattle's never been a pretty thing. But it's become, in the era of agribusiness, horrendous, with livestock hearing and smelling the deaths in front of them, often falling to the ground to be dragged to the slaughter—or failing to be properly stunned, so they may be dismembered as they live. The ranks of the autistic grow, and I want to say it's part of the modern age of technologized pain that perhaps we need more of those who can give a simple, intestinal response. Though I know that's romanticizing evolution.

Or think of hyperactive Ted Nelson with his hummingbird mind. Van Gogh in the asylum with color pouring out of him, as the rise of industrialization painted the skyline gray. Poor depressed Abraham Lincoln, on suicide watch.

My friend Dawn says, "It's like they need us, you know?" (shaking her blond hair, a young mother taught by gorillas to make the pain grimace called a "smile" in human culture). "Like we're filters for all the emotional shit that's out there."

Comings has a habit of using the term *pedigree* to refer to families; he'll list a mother and father who have, say, depression and Tourette's respectively, then say, "Of this pedigree come . . ." and tick off flawed children, grandchildren. I suppose he would not consider Bruce's a good pedigree, or mine, or Dawn's, or Jin's either probably—young, impulsive, rule-breaking birth parents, tainted chromosomes all.

I WANT TO SEE this impossible future. It is on the one hand a litter. The same homogocene we step into no matter what: the crows that have evolved into shovel-beaked diggers and webfoot swimmers and even songbirds with jeweled heads and titanium-white backs. Cockroaches that have become small birds, and the thousand species of grass. Perhaps we're no longer masters of this domain but comical sidekicks to it. What lumes our eyes is the fierce light of intelligence—or will—shutting off. Some of us bang our heads all day long on the decaying walls of houses long since torched or hacked or neglected, eroding with us in this future of impulsivity, violence. Maybe the criminal among us will have demolished the borders of zoos, and predators, multiplying, will be back among us, finding us easy targets. They will compete with us for the top niche again. A man speaking gibberish *lalalalalalalala* flops in a leopard's mouth. It's the leopard, now, whose scourge will be the intelligent machine.

ONCE, at a place where we camp in the summer—a former ashram, a cheap place in the San Juan Islands—I saw a woman drop a small beaded bag on a chair while she took pictures. A nearby crow swooped it up as soon as her back was turned, flying to the roof of a cabin and dropping it so it slid down the roof into the gutter, chain hanging down a little bit. Then the crow hopped to a nearby branch and watched until the woman came back. She grabbed for her beaded bag and searched with mounting hysteria, finally glimpsing the chain and heading off for a ladder.

The crow throughout the scene watched intently, uttering little caws.

Is there a moment, in our Big Bang of the mind, when we developed mockery?

I'm a crow lover, or at least crow watcher. I listen to them and know their sounds and imagine in the future I could make a kind of rude communication. Maybe these evolved crows take me and show me the giant Douglas firs where they've pecked out, with pollens and berries mixed with ash, murals of the human. Ocher, charcoal, queasy with movement. Enormous: walls and walls of us flying, almost horizontal, almost pre-bipedal, arms and legs released from gravity.

Or I can see a different future. Maybe we're drifting away from, or learning how to end, our existence as top predators. Our new genetically shifting selves are far from the calculating minds that can systematically destroy species. We're nonverbal and alive with pictures, or predatory in clumsy ways. And now and again, in this world, we might find in our changed selves a new survival.

LEAR'S DAUGHTER complained that he "hath ever but slenderly known himself." Whom did she compare him with, I wonder? Herself? Did she see herself as a top predator, a barely conscious primate grasping at resources? Did she *know herself*?

Evolution, as we've learned it in the past, moves slowly and peacefully forward, like grass making its way through the digestive system of a cow. At the end it will be milk, foaming and useful. In the gullet of time, change comes without a glimpse. Looking at the human timeline, we can see instead a frenzied telescoping of change: 100,000 years as Homo sapiens, 50,000 years as the linguistic, symbolic creatures we are, 10,000 years of settlements, then a few hundred years of industrialization and the mad rush of the twentieth century, beginning with horse-drawn carriages and ending with nuclear weapons and artificial brains.

We are, I think, learning finally who and what we are. Maybe it's the genome project, maybe it's cloning. Almost 2,000 years after he wrote, we're all becoming Augustinians, puzzling out time, thought, and humanity. We telescope into seeing ourselves, Homo sapiens sapiens. Who are we, who've remade the entire planet? Often melancholy, writing endings that only become new work. We have chosen to define ourselves by our consciousness, but when we examine this consciousness it flickers away, a bare speck of what makes us act. We define ourselves, perhaps, by what is pointless and ineffectual about us, as if we were to say our vestigial tailbone makes us human.

I wonder if we're moving toward nothing at all, or a day when we can use the bit of consciousness we have to change.

AUGUSTINE ASKED, bewildered, *What do I love when I love You?*

Because here's the thing: me, a primate, a top predator, using this convention that I'm just a voice. Occasionally I tease you, reader, by telling you what I'm doing. To speak to you, unknown but curious predator lushly centered in this world we've made over in our image: this piece of time called the homogocene, the human world.

Patchily furred, easily cold, but javelin-toothed we are. In these linguistic spaces we butt consciousnesses, easily, like horned sheep, and break apart. Really we are warm—nearly one hundred degrees, radiant—sleepy, hungry. At times what brings me here comes from the brain stem: a gut fear of my own life. It's not cortical, this fear: it's australopithecine, it climbs from the silt.

It seems wrong in me to love these primates as much as I do. *My bad,* as they say now: my sin. Augustine, you have not saved me; I have a love of created things, at least two. Mornings I lie under the daisy-pegged quilt I helped patch and embroider, using a sewing needle, a tool invented 26,000 years ago. They are with me, my primates, my top predators; I stroke their heads, one head dark and sculpted by the pillow into storm cloud, one dark and straight as rain. They remind me consciousness is not a kind of torture or a wrecking-power, but a skiff that allows my hand to skim sweet waters.

My palm rests on my son's cheek as I watch his profile, the mouth open, round nose mimicking my thumb. Even on waking, his breath is good. At four he regards me, his mother, as the world's finest predator. I bring him what he desires. We lie under the quilt, restlessly butting our limbs together for the warmth, knowing we have to go out there sometime.

In my Libet-mind I have loved them ten times longer than I've loved them.

In the morning, while Bruce and I read the paper, my son absorbs cartoons. His favorite one's about a Stone Age family who wear leopard clothing and live in a stone house alongside apatosauruses, saber-toothed cats, triceratops, all beasts separated by their extinctions, all really living millions of years apart.

"Watch with me!" he says when I pick up the paper. He can't stand to do anything alone (we're social creatures, herd mammals after all), and I don't mind—on the screen I see the view of the world imagined by Saint Bernard of Clairvaux, the divine world in which the ages have not come and gone but exist together. Coeternal, survivable, playing out in front of me in waves of electromagnetic energy, as I lie under the Neanderthal grave of the quilt.

Though I have to send him out in the world after all— Augustine, he's only three feet tall, the size of *Homo floresiensis,* with no new place to walk, no end. He has only a green, pink, and blue blanket named Fuzzy to keep him. The earth is swarming, literally swarming. Augustine: What dust will we use, when we make ourselves?

PANDEMONIUM
ON ZOMBIE EARTH

ONCE, a decade ago or longer, Bruce came home to find me on the front steps of our house, crying. Actually, he came home because I called him at the university where he taught as a graduate assistant and told him my brain was on fire. When he got home and asked me why I was crying, I told him I couldn't go into the house because it was filled with poison gas. I kept telling him my brain was burning up, which I believed then was literally true. I was, he tells me, completely terrified and disoriented. He bundled me up and took me to my doctor, a lovely woman I still miss, who tried to talk me into going to the hospital, but I didn't, and she gave me lots of major drugs. After a while I realized my house was filled with nothing but the same particulate-tinged air everyone breathes on the Eastern Seaboard.

I was too out of touch; we can't have a world in which everyone weeps in doorways all the time. So I put pills down my throat and make sure I don't weep in doorways; nothing that severe has happened to me in more than a decade. Not where I became incoherent and couldn't talk about—couldn't deal with—what was happening to me. Still we live in our conceivable worlds, in our fictions, in what philosopher Thomas Metzinger calls all of our "subjective universes" butting together. There we somehow forget our algae-laced future, volatile organic compounds, nitrogen oxides, carbon monoxide rotating into those hungry alveoli. These we lose, in the conceivable future we make together.

"WE'RE POISED on a lotta knife edges right now," says Thor. He's says this lounging on a pillowed deck chair, looking not at all like a man on the edge of a blade. He lounges very convincingly, in fact, with his sprawly, comfortable body. I've asked him to speculate on the future.

"Well, in eight hundred years eighty percent of the earth's biota will be gone," he says, adding that we're near another glacial age. "I can see a future of monoculture, a huge population, every bit of space taken up growing something simple like algae to feed ourselves."

That picture flickers in my mind, many billions of us, jammed in like spoons in a drawer, eating soup plates of anchovy-stinking frill.

Many knife edges. Poised. Thor adds this casually. I guess we've always been on some sort of knife edge, with our brief 10,000-year warmings between ice ages (our present one due to end now, a knife edge), our plagues, our bombs. For a minute I feel my sharp spine as an imprint of my species history, a reminder. We have just watched a river otter dismember a crab. Claw by claw went the otter, pausing to eat, the crab's remaining claws waving as the otter ripped along. Slow as a greeting, as if to say, dying's not such a big deal, not enough to disrupt the normal courtesies.

And perhaps, I have to consider, I am part of a trend that's speeding the end of humanity along.

THE SOUR ME'S FADING, though, on a day when even dismemberment's polite: Thor's relaxed body and spoonlike spine, big enough to fill a long and important lounge chair, our talk on the glassed-in porch of a house lavished with wood and light, built over a stretch of private beach on one of the San Juan Islands. Paradox comes as easily these days as supermarket dinners: *Minute Rice, Suddenly Salad, Irony Helper.* These two houses I visit belong to friends who have far more human resources at their disposal than I have, and I'm loving the illusion of luxury. No poison gases here, and we have not been eating plates of algae. Each of the four families staying here has brought several meals, and for lunch today someone roasted a pork loin, and put it out with French bread, cheese, and fruit.

This part of the island is named Lonesome Cove. When we're not eating our large, intricate, carnivorous meals, we go down to the beach, or hike, or chat together on the porch. I imagine that if you took that 50,000-year trip to the beginning of consciousness, we could be the best-situated human tribe, sitting lazily in our large cave, roasting reindeer in fat drenched with sweet calories, walking by the water.

I've dragged with me my consciousness books and read in

Merlin Donald a statement that seems written for this weekend: "After two million years of evolution, the existence of elaborate experience industries testifies to our infinite strangeness."

We produce or manufacture the experiences we want to have, making the events we want to shiver through our nervous systems—actively, as in arcade rides, or vicariously, as in a film. Donald gives opera as an example, but he could just as easily mention movies, video games, television, even subdivisions, which tend to name themselves after the natural habitat they mow down, giving you the fantasy of living in a place your presence has caused no longer to exist: Cedar Pointe, Eagle Harbor. Perhaps my attachment to a controlled bipolar disorder stems from this need, not so much for manufactured experiences as for constantly changing ones.

"I wish I could be manic-depressive for a little while," Bruce says to me from time to time. "Manic at least. It seems cool in a way."

It is cool in a way. You become, for a moment, the center of the universe again, the bowl into which all of experience is tipped. What you want to do, you can do. I've replanted my garden, thrown great parties, written books in manic fits. I also encounter my splinter selves most sharply. Revising one chapter in this book, I went back to my notes on the page: *she should really take this out,* I had written, about myself.

My manias tend to end in spikes of paranoia and doom— poison gas in the house, bullets whizzing in the air—the condition is a sword you fall upon eventually.

But I expect, to get things done, or just to live differently, I allow mild mania to happen. As we all make our experience: *Your*

Thursdays begin at 8 o'clock, says an ad for an evening's TV lineup, in case we forget our lives center in manufactured experience. Before eight o'clock we're dull, rote, unalive creatures. Neanderthals.

This weekend is a made experience for the group. There are some twenty-one of us, with grown kids, teenagers, my Jin, a grandmother. We have choreographed the sunset vistas and the banquets of bird and haunch and the visits to the tide pools. Except for the hosts, we live in the made experience of having this chunk of the earth's bounty for ourselves, a dizzy fantasy sweeping me through the weekend: where my study would be in this house, how my thin Savannah would weave through the rocks. It's maybe a testimony to our infinite strangeness that nothing in our manufactured experience slips out of tone by talk of our current extinctions. Our bodies, which decide what dreads to feel, stay becalmed. ("The speed at which species are being lost is much faster than any we've seen in the past—including those [extinctions] relating to meteor collisions." Who said that? Daniel Simberloff.)

"It'll suck for our great-great-whatever-great-grandchildren," says Thor. "Anyway, I won't be there, eating algae" (a man named for the Norse creator-god of thunder), and I won't either, and that's how our conversation ends.

I COME ACROSS this from cognitive scientist Ivan Havel: "We [humans] can think about the conceivable and the real blended together into one conceivable world."

Or as Lewis Carroll put it in *Through the Looking Glass:*

"If you'll believe in me, I'll believe in you. Is that a bargain?" said the Unicorn.

"Yes, if you like," said Alice.

My conceivability now is living in these two enormous houses with beachfront, worth more than I'll earn in my lifetime. My weekend's waking dream—a typical slice of human consciousness—reflects no rejection of my real home, the small place I love ferociously and that coinhabits my mind then, weedy herb garden, ancient wavy glass, half my neighbor's weeping silver birch, and all. My real life, so tangible to me I am barely aware of thinking it, loses nothing and exists as an undercurrent in my imagined one, neither bothering the other.

BEFORE 50,000 YEARS AGO, William Calvin writes, humans lived in the "long childhood" of dwelling in the present.

So we have two human times: one the time before consciousness of past and future—and so in a real sense *without* past and future—and one the time of conceivability, rote of living and thick frosting of pretend. Where you turn into your Eagle Pointe and dream the eagles, your Spyglass Place and watch for marauding ships. And this is humanity at its most normal.

MY BOY CURLS into my chest: I look down at him, loving the back of his head, the wedge of straight hair cropped across, leaving that tender empty space of flesh behind each ear: haircut gaps that in a little boy seem to hold the movement from babyhood to full frail humanity: the skull of childhood yielding its vulnerable space.

Of course I love his head, too, the way it swells above the neck, fleshy ears poked out a bit, one lobe dented in the middle. I love all of him—his long legs, kink of a spine, rectal puck with its little ring of rejectamenta. I love him in my bowels; they stir with love, unable, in their fleshness, to refuse to love any part of him. My mind sleeps in the expansive content of my intestinal loving. Which aches if I try to think about it, a warning that my heart's a basted thing, a brief sewing that can rip apart.

I wonder if as a manic-depressive I can love more than others do; it feels that way, in this complete almost hyperfocused acceptance of him, this stretching to the crazy limits of what I can feel. I recognize the self-aggrandizement of parents, at least those who've given over most of their lives to their children, and I guess I'm probably indulging in it. But for Bruce, too. My brain burning. Ah, this love.

THOMAS METZINGER writes something that staggers me as I look at my son: "Within each of us a cosmos of consciousness unfolds temporarily, a subjective universe develops. The first part of the problem is to understand how such a variety of subjective universes can constantly form and disappear in our objective universe."

My son's four now, very conscious, a boy who's traveled through human history, from australopithecine toddlerhood to human now, a child of wonder and conceivability, who assumes a part like Harry Potter and stays in character for weeks. The *future* still hard to conjure, in his subjective space: "tomorrow tomorrow" is the best we can do for communicating the day after tomorrow to him, "back" for the past. A universe in twenty-four-hour orbit. He still needs me to lead him into the planet's larger spinning— When is Christmas? When is summer?—and I get to hold him, in the systole and diastole of joy. With a slip of me that names it "joy," in addition to feeling its pulse.

Does that voice, created to throw a javelin, hold that word? Is *it* happy? I remember watching a group of Tibetan monks create a sand mandala, a four-foot circle of intricate spirals and geometries, made by pouring colored grains from a funnel all day for a week, four monks working in slow, chronic movements like automata.

"To quiet the mind," they said. Then they swept it up, to remind us all that life ends quickly.

UNLESS THE AIR'S GORGED with fog and rain, as it can be around here, I see the San Juan Islands every day. If I walk to the end of my street I can see them, along with a bald eagle who nests in a tree down there; Jin calls him Grif. I hear the barking of the slow, modular-sofa-like sea lions. The islands catch at me as tragedy does: stepping off to the horizon, the near ones knuckled and khaki and the far ones humped shades. I see them as drowned mountains, which they are. Glaciers reamed this valley during the last ice age, followed in retreat by a rush of water. The tips of these volcanic peaks show like lids, over downed trees—hemlock and cedar—iced fur, ground beaks, and blued feather. Like the eclipsed moon, the mountains in their dress appear beautiful and nauseating. It's again, perhaps, my sickness to see this way. Though it's not a conceivable world but the real one.

My world of poison gas and burning organs was a conceivable world or subjective universe, medicated away to a different subjectivity. That new one allows for the fresh tragedy of million-year-old drowned mountains.

At another time I'll go to teach temporarily in the state of Iowa, and write to Dawn about all the roadkill on Iowa highways. Skunks, squirrels, cats, groundhogs, deer, raccoons lie in those grotesque stuffed-animal postures, smeared, spreading. Jin and I on our walks find broken-off beaks, paws.

God, I couldn't live there, Dawn writes. When I talk to her about it on a visit home, she tears up. Again, this is not the subjective world but the world itself. I can't find many people in Iowa who notice.

AS A CHILD I entered astonishing fugue states, walking in front of cars, staring with such an unblinking not-thereness I got mistaken for a blind, begging child. It may have been petit mal seizures; one doctor made that diagnosis. Sometimes I had no idea where I'd gone. Other times I was aware of a deep daydreaming or a deep level of thought—as in my existential trip to the candy store—that left no room for processing the present.

There's no real ending to the story of my days on the drowned mountain, hiking on those humps of it spared from flood. I can tell you the couple whose house we stayed at are no longer friends, not because of anything we did but because of a falling-out with other friends of ours. That's okay; we humans are a tribal species, prone to division. I can add that the woman half of the couple had changed her name to Peace and believes ardently in fairies. Neither behavior's strange around here: we know people named Butterfly, Everyhope, a mother named Rainy Day whose daughter's name is Stormy, Gaia, Bliss, Krishna. If you ask people they'll tell you they've taken on "good karma" names. Some wear their subjective universes closer to the skin than others.

ONE PERSISTENT THEORY of autism—I would call it a bias—holds that autistics have no "theory of mind," defined as the ability to recognize or infer the mental life of another person. No theory of mind, the thinking goes, leads to lack of empathy. Many clinicians still believe this. Autistics argue they may develop a theory of mind later than neurotypicals, but the compensation for this later development is a theory of mind that's far more sophisticated, that recognizes the uniqueness of each individual's mental life. Neurotypical theory of mind tends to infer the mental state of others by following the rules of one's own. As one clinician puts it, the autistic may rely on a not-like-me awareness of the other, rather than a like-me awareness. A contributor to the Institute for the Neurologically Typical addresses theory of mind this way: the neurotypical theory of mind is that everyone thinks like me, while the neuroatypical theory would be that everyone's mind is "vastly and mysteriously" different from my own.

"Have you ever noticed that 'normal' people cannot think about the possibility that each person might live in a separate world?" he asks.

The man who wrote the Amazon review of my friend Dawn's book had a like-me awareness, shaken up by her radically different mind ways.

I have not polled normal people to see whether or not they can think this. I know it has been clear to me since childhood, when each set of eyes that passed me, including those of my closest family, seemed like windows in a jetliner taking off, never clearly visible and becoming invisible in no time at all.

MY THEORY of mind is one of not-me-ness. It causes me to stare and behave in ways I probably shouldn't, and makes the act of writing irresistible—the chance to bring that alien universe out there in touch with my own, if only for a second. Perhaps this is the meme that infects us with the sense that UFOs are trying to reach us, directing whales to our shores. In some way, the meme of the distance between intelligences—our need to recognize it and stretch across—may be one of those memes Preti and Miotto would say we need. The eyes I see around me do not reflect back to me anything I feel sure I can know. The boy down the street dreams in his subjective universe, his experience industry, of killing and opening a smaller boy. When he sees vulnerabilities of the flesh he sees something quite different from what I see: a frog on a high school lab table, an envelope, a book that fell into his lap. It sickens me but doesn't surprise me, somehow.

I don't feel I can know in any real way those I love the most, my husband and my son. If I were granted one vision, I've always thought, I'd most want to see my son as a grown-up, content. With me or away from me: though I'd want the resentment all children feel for their mothers—particularly mothers who uproot them and soothe them with songs of drowning—to be out-weighed by the love he feels. I would want him to think of my face.

THE CHILD in my arms lies facedown, his back under my hands to massage or scratch lightly. I'm scratching, and also thinking of cognitive theorists George Lakoff and Mark Johnson, who pin human behavior at about 95 percent unconscious. Unconscious programs called demons do our mental work. This cognitive model, called the "pandemonium model," came from neurosci-entist Oliver Selfridge in 1959; the metaphor he borrows is of the cacophonous demons in *Paradise Lost*. Minor demons in your cra-nium yell and scream, vying for the attention of more powerful action demons, who finally use their authority to have a hand get the phone, or scratch the suede back of a child. Still, you don't hear them. Unless you're afraid of your creditors or your neigh-bor's tuna casserole, you don't think about a ringing phone. You answer it. You drive familiar places barely knowing how you got there. At the end of each year on New Year's Eve you flop into a chair and say, That was a year, that's gone. While the refrigerator does its Morse-code ticking, stairs creak, whatever, your demons flank you. You sit quiet in your sheltered wedge of the castle, the lonely prince.

A school of consciousness theorists, consciousness inessen-tialists, believe that consciousness is an evolutionary side product; we're driven by unconscious behavior, and consciousness, in a pointless way, rides along, talking. We could do without it; we could just as easily be zombies, living on a zombie earth. It's just my luck that my consciousness happens to talk louder and on more channels than others' some of the time, and in a more *What's the point of it all?* way the rest of the time. Both sides— essentialism and inessentialism—have a lot of adherents in philosophy and the cognitive sciences. Some conscious inessentialists offer hedges, like that consciousness does give us the ability to philosophize about having consciousness, kvetch about our position in the world—as if consciousness might be thrown in as a neurological form of the experience industry, something to entertain us as we live.

I THINK ABOUT all this and don't think, another human body laid out in front of me, smaller and smoother than my own, and without the scars that have become my personal universe's atmosphere. My Selfridge demons hold me in the moment, safe from things like the feel of each of the couch's fake fibers, the distinct thunk of horse chestnuts hitting the ground outside, our street's one squirrel (in a town that did not have squirrels ten years ago) chittering.

The body's here, too (with its own demons?), this intense love that seems to live in the torso, beginning almost in the chest and deepening in the lowness, the places of food and liquid and blood loading up with survival. At various times in history people have located the center of the body in the heart and the liver. In certain cultures the brain's been considered a vestigial organ.

We love guts in my house. The last time I had surgery, one summer ago, I had my surgeon give me photos. Jin found them one day in a drawer next to our dining table and we looked at them together, him in my lap, seeing what lay behind the pillow of padded skin that held him.

What's that? he asked, pointing to a scalpel that held up, in display, a white, wet ovary, tugging it from the womb. What is that *doing* there?

Almost like birth, revised: he may not have lulled his way into form in my uterus, but now he knows more of it than any womb-born child would, the wet saturated-pink surface etched with magenta veins, gluey fallopian tombs. Marcus Aurelius writes that the sole life we can lose is the one that we live at this moment, and we can have no other life than that which we lose: so the longest life, and the shortest, amount to the same. Live to be a hundred, die at birth: just a few heartbeats etch you in the glass of the living. Scratching a child's back.

PARADISE EARTH

M Y STAY IN IOWA CITY, when it comes, feels loaded
with spiritual yearning, the promise of Eden, and loss—
the Mormons departing from this place with their handcarts, the
Amish towns and True Inspirationist Amana Colonies, Vedic City
and the roadkill. I realize I normally live cocooned by my friends,
whom I love, and who to a greater or lesser degree don't mind
my quirks. Now it's just me, Bruce, Jin, and the roadkill. So we
arrange to go visit my brother and Olivia and N'Lili at my
brother's house in Minneapolis. I love them and feel they don't
mind my quirks, so whenever I think about going to see them,
I get weepy. I've been getting weepy a lot, and writing a lot,
and feeling twitchy; probably a bit hypomanic, or a little below
full mania.

We drive on a stretch of interstate known as the Avenue of
the Saints. Formal blue signs declare this to be the Avenue of the

Saints, just as other signs tell us we're passing the town with the largest frying pan in the state of Iowa, the Spam Museum, in Minnesota.

Living near Amish country has reminded me of N'Lili's attempts to exist physically as a woman, in Amish country, somewhere in the Midwest. ("I dressed up in full drag. I thought I looked great," she told me. "Then I went to a restaurant and everybody just turned around and stared.") I haven't seen Olivia and N'Lili in a year, though we've talked on the phone and exchanged e-mail messages a lot, especially me and N'Lili: me to them, me to one in particular.

THE MORE CURRENT TERM for multiple personality is *dissociation,* though dissociation is a behavioral spectrum, with normal dissociation—"zombie" behavior, forgetting how you drive your car to work—at one end, and the extreme personality splitting of someone like N'Lili, who functions or has functioned as separate individuals for most of her life, at the other. Unlike bipolar disorder or autism, this type of dissociation appears to have little to do with fundamental genetic wiring of the brain, although it's associated with intelligence: a creative, smart response to an overwhelming situation. The therapeutic response is to strive for integration, the personalities drawn together, eventually, into a unified whole. It isn't always what patients want. Some multiples want to be considered as different people who happen to be sharing one body, and these people, like so many others nowadays, draw on the language of personhood—in this case, for their selves—to frame this need. N'Lili does try for a certain degree of integration but has also made peace with her remaining personalities.

Integrating a personality into the others, never seeing her again, involves a "terrible grieving" process, she tells me (it also can mean a name change; when I first met N'Lili, she was Nettie). Once, a personality named Tani, a poet, a painter, highly emotional and always in love, decided she was a "hindrance" to the group. "She could not control her emotions, and the thought of a life consisting of ever-present restraints, a psychological straitjacket, was unendurable," N'Lili wrote to me in a letter. "But rather than let her go as a misfit or unloved—we created an enchanted and enchanting assisted suicide." In the center of an Enchanted Forest inside N'Lili, on a stump called the Home Free Tree, singing all the other girls out from the forest to be with her (almost two hundred finally appeared), Tani died.

While that process of losing someone hurts, the work N'Lili does, to hold the remaining group together and keep them in harmony, is difficult, too. One personality she has now, Naomi, is a vegetarian, so they've all had to become vegetarian in order to accommodate her, in order to go out together and go into a restaurant and eat. And though the personalities do work hard to accommodate one another, they still aren't always aware of one another's actions.

N'LILI'S A HUSKY GUY, fifty-five years old, with sparkly studs along the ears, big shoulders, broad calves, and white hair pulled back in a ponytail. (Talking on the phone recently, she told me, "I bought your mom an earring to match my earring. I guess your mom and I are going steady.") Blue eyes, good, strong, broad features, but not feminine ones. Nevertheless she's female, and mostly young. N'Lili and Olivia were married by a justice of the peace, and they removed all gender language from their ceremony. N'Lili doesn't call my cousin "wife." I slip on all this language, still.

"Just say 'person,' " she tells me a lot, gently.

I first met my cousin Olivia, daughter of my mother's younger brother, when she was six and moved to the United States, to New Jersey, from England with her family, where my uncle had had a job and she spent her younger childhood. She's a bit over a year younger than me but has always been much braver, and predictably became both my favorite playmate and one of the children in my extended family I felt most jealous of. ("Daddy likes her much better than me," I wrote in my diary. "He's disappointed I'm not pretty.")

When Olivia was six and seven years old, I read to her down at our family's shore cottage from a book of gruesome fairy tales housed there. In her favorite, "Jack the Giant Killer," Jack escapes from the giant by persuading the giant to slit his own stomach open with a sword. I had to read that story to her again and again and again.

In my mind she exists both ways, though we're in our forties: as the adult woman who's lightened her hair and married N'Lili, and the black-haired girl sucking her thumb and demanding to hear again about the slit-stomached giant who kept a roomful of human arms and legs for snacking on.

"Read that part again," she said, her thumb a pulsing extension of her upper lip. "The arms-and-legs one."

Olivia always has been very pretty. She's somewhat dark, with features that tend to the Greek, inherited from her Greek mother. As a child, when we played together at the shore, she directed our outdoor games of Fort and indoor games of Risk and go-go danced, the center of attention while I wore my patented look of affliction off in someone's armchair. She gave me horror stories to read, about invasions of flesh-eating batwinged creatures called Berbalangs, and rolled over and went to sleep while I quivered in the dark. Nevertheless she's smart and incredibly funny and still very pretty and impossible to stay away from. Her laugh's one of the most infectious things I know.

"I love you guys," says N'Lili, when we tumble into Minneapolis hours late because of traffic. "I mean really. Out of all proportion to the amount of time I spend with you." She's like that, saying things if she thinks them.

My brother Chris tries very hard to feed us chicken marsala and pasta with eggplant, in spite of the fact that we caved in on the way and stopped at a diner. Olivia's laughing. Her large tattooed spouse in the rough cloth of a male body is a woman. I don't need to know why Olivia's laughing.

They are just so much my people. My tribe. A new place brings with it a pressure toward normalcy. There's no one in Iowa City to talk to about word aversions or the astonishing amount of roadkill Iowa makes, as if the asphalt itself tosses up bodies. Someone else has had to function for me. Now it's safe; I can do what I want. We're busting out of my brother's small house; you practically expect to see joists pop. Bruce, Jin, and I sleep in one room we fill from wall to wall; Olivia and N'Lili take the living room in air mattress and couch (Chris offered them his room but N'Lili has trouble with closed-in spaces, even declining to sit with her back to the door in restaurants).

ONE OF THE religious communities near Iowa City—besides the Amish towns and a city based on the teachings of the Maharishi Mahesh Yogi, Vedic City—consists of a group of seven villages called the Amana Colonies, founded by German religious persecutees who called themselves the Church of the True Inspiration. The colonists came to Iowa in 1855 after a brief stay in Buffalo, New York, and remained communal until 1932. They worked together in the gardens and the fields and ate the same meals together in long communal kitchens. Religious leaders called *werkzeug* led the Amanas, speaking in direct unpredictable prophecy from God to the people, so that the *werkzeug* had to be accompanied everywhere by scribes. I've been to Amana and seen the diaries of the scribes recording the *werkzeug*. *My foot is seldom seen openly,* God scolded the people once.

I WOULD LOVE to travel somewhere, as the colonists or the Mormons did, at a prophet's command. As it is, I've traveled to see my family, whom I miss. All too human. We arrive in Minneapolis late and have a little chat, complain about the hours of stop-and-start driving. Then Olivia lays out her air mattress, blows it up, rolls over, and goes to sleep in the middle of the living room.

"It's just what you used to do to me with the Berbalangs," I tell her, but she's past caring. Turns out, after scaring the bejesus out of me back then, she can't remember Berbalangs, or any of her other fiends.

In the morning N'Lili's setting the table, putting out croissants and Italian bread. She tends to gravitate to the kitchen, anyone's kitchen; she wipes; she grabs your dishes when you're done. Jin's been up all night with nightmares and we're all exhausted, three lumps. N'Lili's been up since five o'clock, walking along the Mississippi River. She's crackling with energy, putting us to shame. I feel as though I could plug a toaster into her.

Today we're going to the Minnesota State Fair. My brother's always wanted to take us there, to see the queen of the State Fair, Princess Kay of the Milky Way, carved in butter. Every year he goes to the fair and calls us to report on Princess Kay, a State Fair institution since 1954, the year Chris was born. Every year the fair features this succession of women renamed Kay and given pride of place in the heavens, like the mistresses of gods: slender women carved in cold, congealed fat.

N'Lili wants to go to the fair just as badly, because this year some of the original Munchkins from *The Wizard of Oz* will be there. So this voyage, too, is a pilgrimage.

We six keep jostling over the one bathroom.

"Let's go," says N'Lili. "The Munchkins are only there until two."

We're trying to leave but someone always needs to go to the bathroom, or Jin runs out and discovers some neighbor boy and he's off.

"Look, I could just go and meet you there," says N'Lili, getting nervous. I have never seen so clearly all the little girls— Peggy, I suppose, in the lead, vibrant and smitten with *The Wizard of Oz.* She can't wait to get out the door, hovering there, smearing sunscreen on her fair, brawny, and tattooed arms.

"I'll go wherever you guys want to go but I just hate stuff like this," grumbles Olivia. I'm mostly dying to see the butter woman, Princess Kay, though I'm uneasy for my sleep-deprived son, who hates heat, hates crowds, hates rides. We take a neighbor and a few neighborhood boys along to try to keep him happy.

N'LILI RADIATES HAPPINESS. A kind of settled but jolly contentment rolls off her in waves. I remarked on this as soon as we got to Minneapolis: *You just seem so happy.* She sat on the couch, smoothing a hand over her short white ponytail, ankle propped on knee, a comfortable and amiable group of females. She, too, is a commune: always, beyond our hearing, in the midst of the endless negotiations communes must have to survive. Will we serve meat? Will we sit over here or over there? Very few communes last. Amana, with eighty years of communal living, was unusually successful, but ultimately many colonists wanted to make their own choices and eat their own meals. N'Lili, sewed into a single skin, has no such options.

I'm happier than I've ever been in my life, she told me.

Why?

Years of work and therapy. N'Lili said this radiantly laughing.

I HAVE BEEN THINKING about happiness a lot lately. Perhaps because Jin has been unhappy and his unhappiness sits in my gut. I worry about what it takes to make him, or any of us, happy. We live surrounded by evidence of people who subjected themselves to unimaginable hardships, Mormons hitching themselves to their own goods and hauling them 1,700 miles to Utah—their paradisical place of Deseret—lying down to sleep in the singing fury of the tallgrass prairie. A healthy number of them died. As I imagine the Amanans did on the trek here to Iowa, to work all day and eat silently at sex-segregated tables in their communal dining halls, sauerkraut put up over the winter, oat soup. All of them aiming toward that joy everlasting.

And N'Lili radiantly laughing. And Jin so miserable, not making this transition well, to Iowa City. He's a social little guy and at home trails through the neighborhood with a cloak of friends. Here he's met only a few other boys, and his school's filling him with anxiety about things like his poor handwriting. Last night he screamed and screamed in his sleep, having a night terror; he sat up flailing and screaming that he'd never have the *bestest handwriting* and for half an hour he screamed pitifully for his *Mommy!*, though I lay right there holding him, hard.

His eyes liquid in the dark, terrified and not seeing me at all. Arms and legs flailing. It was awful. Finally he woke up and I stayed with him, on his air mattress with the Thomas the Tank Engine sheets my brother had bought him, until he slept again. I eased back into my own bed, squeezed up to his; he half-woke, demanded that I sleep with my arm hanging down so he could grasp my hand periodically. My arm turned lifeless, a baseball bat hanging from the bed.

AT THE FAIR N'Lili charges off to the Munchkins almost as soon as we get there; the boys howl past a misery's worth of Sno-Kones and cotton candy. She's gotten a map of the fair and leads us through it like Sherman on the march, though the place is hot, and huge, and mobbed. This is Labor Day weekend and the temperature's in the nineties somewhere; it's buggy and humid. And in spite of N'Lili's considerable determination, chunks of us keep breaking off and getting lost. At one point the boys go off on a river ride and we don't know where it gets out; Bob, the neighbor, goes to chase the boys; Chris goes to find Bob; N'Lili wanders off to find a hat; Olivia just wanders off.

Olivia stands in the shade. "This is just my idea of *hell*," she keeps telling me. Like Jin, she hates rides, hates heat, hates crowds.

I HAVE BEEN HAUNTING the Amana Colonies. I am fascinated by the Church of the True Inspiration, by the handwriting of the scribes taking down the word of God. It would not fascinate me so much if the colonies weren't still inhabited by people who seem, by and large, to feel they *are* living in paradise. This obsesses me, and my obsession begins to wear off on Bruce. We go there a lot; we get invited to a communal dinner, something the seven villages still have periodically. When I go to the Amanas I ask questions of as many residents as I can find.

Look, a woman tells me one day. We have no crime. None. It's weird—we get biker gangs coming through here and they won't even put a cigarette out on the ground.

Don't you ask yourselves why another *werkzeug* hasn't appeared? I say.

A lot of the colonists believe, she answers, that they existed to lead us to paradise, and now we're here and we don't need them anymore.

If we need one, she continues, he or she will come.

ALWAYS, if my boy wakes up in the night, I have trouble sleeping. Even the sound of a bird landing on a twig can heave me out of sleep, fearing for him. I sleep lightly and wake often. The night before the fair, I got Jin back to sleep around 3 or 4 A.M. and then woke up every hour or so. Jin and Bruce both breathed that slow, true breath of rest, the air going tender. Each time I listened and went back under ecstatic. I'm not saying I want Jin to have night terrors. Not that at all.

THE MUNCHKINS ARE at the other side of the State Fair—a good walk, as it turns out. N'Lili keeps offering to go on her own and meet us somewhere, but we've made a decision to stay together; meeting up seems like it would be tough in this mob, with its currents and countercurrents, and we're talking a mile a minute, in between dodging people who wear cheese hats and eat food-on-a-stick. My brother's warned me ahead of time that everything at the State Fair's served on a stick: there's Cajun chicken on a stick, pork chop on a stick, corn on a stick. Fried Twinkies. On a stick.

When the boys whine too much we say, We'll put you on a stick and set up a stand and sell you.

The Munchkins sit at a booth at the back of one of those fair stadiums always filled with booths selling quilts, handmade candles, doilies, juicers. An actress dressed as Dorothy, with heavy, childlike makeup—freckles and wide eyes—keeps the line moving, sells visitors Munchkin photographs from the movie for $30. If you buy the photo, you can get the Munchkins' autographs. There are two actual Munchkins, sitting there on chairs. They've wizened and have grown even smaller with age; they look a bit like dried-apple dolls, expressionless, and overshadowed by the large woman dressed as Dorothy. Unless you buy the photograph, the Munchkins seem primed to pretend you're not there. I'm trying to keep a very unhappy Jin happy, getting him samples of smoothies while N'Lili waits in a moderately long line. When she reaches the front I can hear "N—apostrophe—capital L—no space," as she tries to tell a Munchkin how to spell her name. It takes a while.

N'Lili's quite patient.

"Now I'm happy. Now I don't care what we do. Now I'll just follow you," N'Lili says once she gets her autographed picture, which shows the Munchkins gathering around the ankles of Judy Garland's Dorothy. N'Lili will take out the photograph, holding it lovingly and admiring it, for the rest of the day, then display it on Chris's mantelpiece.

JIN IS NOT HAPPY. At least not right now, at the State Fair. Nothing at the fair interests Jin in the least. So I just decide to hang it up and look at the things I'm interested in, and then I feel guilty about that.

I want to see Princess Kay, who presides over an innocent galaxy of dairy products.

Picture a large glass cylinder or vault, like a glass cage. In it a small chair, a knife. Nine heads rotate on an outer ring, like something strange dropped from Saturn's atmosphere, though the heads are Barbie-like in their femininity. Each in fact has almost the same features—straight, long nose, pert lips, and eyes that seem to aspire to blueness—so the differentiation lies in the hair, chignon, flip, braids. No black or Asian or Native American Princess Kays. Each head is carved from 90 pounds of butter, butter that's quite yellow, and not the best sculpture medium; the jaundiced princesses have thick splots for lashes. The glass cylinder stays cold to keep them from melting to the floor. A new princess gets elected every day of the fair, and at the end one wins the grand title of head princess.

Today's princess has only half emerged from her butter stump; a face perches at the center of the fat globe, features just emerging: long, straight nose, eyes that aspire to blueness. Butter shavings litter the floor. Her sculptor has vanished from his chair for now.

I overhear a conversation behind me as I press up to the glass.

"I knew one of the Princess Kays last year," a woman says. "Name of Ruth Ann Hansen."

"Oh?" Her companion's just a touch interested.

"They give you the head to take home at the end of the fair," her friend plugs on. "The shavings, too. She used them for a few months, on her toast."

I find Chris and Bob, his neighbor, to report this conversation, which we find wildly funny: the head, the weird primacy accorded to toast. (Actually, they both accuse me of making it up. But all I did was change the ex–Princess Kay's name slightly, to protect her eating habits.) As we're talking, today's Princess Kay happens to walk by, her arms loaded with milk shakes.

"Excuse me," my brother says.

"I'm sorry I can't shake hands," she says. She has a long, straight nose, pert lips, eyes that are in fact blue. She seems extremely nice. She assumes we've flagged her down because we want to schmooze with a Princess Kay. "You can shake my elbow."

My brother, with an air of ceremony, shakes her elbow, and says, "Is it true you get to take the sculpture home? Even the shavings?"

"Oh, yeah," she says, juggling her milk shakes.

"What are you going to do with it?" I think Bob asks this.

"I'm going to have a really big corn feed," she says. She smiles radiantly, happy to talk to us about her butter head. "And my little brother's dying to cut off my nose."

"What the hell's a corn feed?" we say later.

Someone volunteers, "I guess you just cook a whole lot of corn."

WE DON'T HAVE a corn feed. We get pizza. N'Lili sits facing the door, and Jin diddles around with his Game Boy. After dinner, I actually get Jin to sleep fairly early, lying down next to him and singing my ballads. Then we break open a bottle of Old Crow bourbon a friend of my brother's dropped off as a gift for Bruce, "one Southerner to another." Chris produces ginger ale. We settle in to bourbon and ginger ale and talk.

"I was never male," N'Lili tells me. "All of us are female. Maleness for me was a social persona. I used it to live in the world."

N'Lili tells me she's been married five times, two times at once. During her periods of complete dissociation she had long black-out periods, waking up in a household in Florida, not knowing what she was doing there, with that family. She has six children and has helped to raise several others. Her adult children now do things like teach grammar school or do costume design. They seem happy. N'Lili and they are close.

"When they understood I was a multiple," she tells us, "they started letting me ride on their backs on our sled." Meaning, I presume, they accepted her as a child, not a large grown man, which seems lovely, and simple.

One of Olivia and N'Lili's habits—you could say eccentricities—is watching the Weather Channel all the time. They've been tussling with Jin over the remote control this weekend—Jin tends to regard visits to relatives as a chance to watch nonstop cartoons—but now with Jin asleep they power the remote safely from their own hands. Hurricane Charlie has just devastated southern Florida, with Hurricane Frances following Charlie by a few days. So the Weather Channel's on, with the Doppler image of whatever hurricane's now destroying retirement community after retirement community, making its slow way across the screen.

We're all refilling our glasses. We're getting into that nostalgic, ripping laughter peculiar to family members with history, the kind of laugh set off by a word, the kind seasoned by some jokes only getting funny years after the event. We're laughing about the night we saw *Jaws* and discovered our little rowboat untethered and I drew the short straw to go get it and a huge dog jumped out of the water; I almost died. We're laughing about

Olivia's father, my Uncle Eddie, who used to keep a hunk of gristle under the kitchen sink and make us kids chew it. (*Better than chewing gum!* he'd roar.) We're laughing about our grim grandfather who never slept.

N'Lili tells us something she's never mentioned before—that she used to think about sex-change surgery, before deciding "to be who I am in this body."

The hurricanes, in the fuzzy spirals of Doppler radar, look like galaxies. Galaxies that approach from the water and extend themselves over the land, able to hold a million worlds just like ours. Or not just like. Cat planets. Bacteria planets. Planets so different only the nonexistent exist. All of them poised to pull the buildings off of the coast of Florida. The news cameras keep focusing in on Vero Beach, the town where my grandfather used to live with his wall of parakeets, being nervous. In these zooms, newscasters reel in front of rain-whipped cameras, pointing to the frantic soda of the shoreline.

N'Lili likes to say, "I'm from another planet anyway."

Would N'Lili choose this mode of being if she had a choice? Is there anything special in it, anything to balance the weight of waking up to a life you don't recognize?

"It is very creative," she says. "I feel full of creative energy."

N'Lili also says that as a multiple, she has no sense of having an unconscious. "I can see everything that's going on in my head. Everything's just laid out in front of me, like a filing cabinet."

We all get pretty looped on Old Crow and ginger ale, laughing, feeling like kids again. It goes on until N'Lili disappears and two-steps back into the room in pajamas, saying, "Somebody's ready to go to bed!"

We go to bed before the end of the State Fair, probably, which extends well into the nighttime. Princess Kay's carved by now, a slim butter head, not the globe of fat with a sprout of features we saw earlier. Still in the center of that revolving ring of heads, like a sun at the center of planets. She's ready to reign in her heaven, looking down on our speared Twinkies and our storms, dripping down on us mortals tears of butter. For our toast.

IT'S A WEEKEND VISIT, so before we know it we have to roll up our stuff from the tiny room and drive home to Iowa City. I miss them practically before we leave. Because we don't want to go, we leave later than we'd planned, though it's about a five-hour drive and Jin's exhausted and needs to go back to regular sleep. We stop for dinner at a pizza place somewhere in Iowa that spells their product *peetsa* and in fact coyly misspells everything. The walls of the restaurant are done in a cheap mural that blends the New York and Chicago skylines into one, and the waiters wear mechanics' overalls. There's an overarching theme here. We don't get it.

On the road Jin plays his Game Boy in the back of the car and Bruce and I discuss evolution. I don't remember how the subject comes up. I know Bruce starts, talking about the uselessness of many-celled organisms like ourselves.

"I don't get evolution," he says, though our track record at the moment is we don't get much of anything. "If prokaryotes like bacteria do so well reproducing themselves, why does evolution bother with a complicated multicelled organism? Why does it bother with something like us?"

Prokaryotes are organisms consisting of just a molecule with a membrane and a cell wall, like simple bacteria. They're notoriously good at survival, sometimes coming back to life after years in a deep freeze, adapting to resist antibiotics. It's hard to find a standard by which they haven't outadapted humans. Eukaryotic life ushers in cell nuclei, mitochondria, ribosomes, organelles, and eventually organs like hearts and spleens and livers—all these avenues of vulnerability. Not to mention the absurd effort involved in it all. Producing something like a human being feels more pointless than carving a classical bust out of butter.

"I just don't get why there need to be eukaryotes at all," says Bruce, with his air of really taking it personally.

"There don't," I tell him. "We're eu-useless."

I'm inordinately pleased with my own humor.

THE THEOLOGICAL ANSWER to why prokaryotic organisms exist is generally *us,* as in, humanity. It's always struck me as rather convenient, asking a critical question and finding out through precious reasoning you yourself are the answer. Us because something divine needs us to serve as mirrors—though what would need 3 billion loopy mirrors is beyond me—or because as the most highly conscious organism (as we think, in our own consciousness, we are), we can create some kind of godhead within ourselves, or because something needs to exist in the animal world that's endowed with free will, something that can be tempted and fall and rise again.

Mormons hold this last belief. They believe we preexist our mortal birth but put on the dress of a body so we can have agency,

can totter our way to God again, where we started. So the birth
of the soul resembles teaching a baby to walk, placing him down
on the floor out of your arms, watching the fleshy legs pump and
fail, scooping him back to where he began. This doctrine has
bounced around in the theology of most Christian faiths.

But to presuppose that God has any need of us—as image, as
chip of light, as infant stumbling in the divine direction—is to
presuppose, it seems to me, that God is not God at all, but something needy, a mother whose breasts swell and ache toward
the child.

WE GOT HOME to Iowa City and two weeks later made one
more pilgrimage. I had wanted as soon as I learned it existed to
go to Vedic City and the Maharishi University of Management fifty
miles away; I read one morning in the newspaper that a peace conference was scheduled there for the following weekend, so we reserved a motel room, got our free registration online—including
vegan lunch—and packed a small suitcase to go.

And here's how we go: passing the huge old mansions in Iowa
City with beer cans in their yards and three Greek letters on their
fronts, nosing the car onto Route 1, through Kalona, where today
a wooden buggy holding an Amish family jiggles by, and the little
boy in his straw boater and the little girl in her black bonnet wave,
and finally arriving at the huge golden domes that mark the campus of the Maharishi University, incarnation of bankrupt old Par-
sons College. You pass a car repair shop called the Quantum
Mechanic and indeed have traveled, like an astronaut of the future,
through time and space.

Vedic City looks both surprisingly sparse—a few dozen buildings spread out on scrubby land—and otherworldly. The houses,
with their long, smooth fronts, pillars, and gold roof ornaments,
are striking, but seem oddly far apart, as if something above flung
them. We take the gravel roads and drive around aimlessly. Several buildings are very imposing: one city-hall-sized structure—
isolated, huge, and gold-leaved in its stubbly plot—declares itself
the Capitol of the Global Country of World Peace.

I feel happy there's a global country of world peace—though
I don't get how it can be both global and a country—but the
enormous building looks depressingly empty.

We can't figure out where to go for this conference, so finally
we pull down a Bradford-pear-lined entry road to the Raj, the spa
that anchors the city and provides Ayurvedic consultations and
treatments. It's also a long, huge building, stately, with the off
note right now of a lighted ambulance in front.

The receptionist is snapping at the ambulance attendants that
the sick patron, whoever it is, "won't go." They shrug and leave
and she snaps into the phone, which she's been hanging on to, "Is
it okay for him to stay? Is it *severe?*"

When the turmoil over the ambulance dies down and we ask
her about the conference, she snaps at us, "I have nothing to do
with that!" and directs us to the university. All of this leaves me
taken aback. I didn't expect anyone around here, meditating and
focused on world peace as I presume they are, to be crotchety.

The mood on campus feels more like what I expected. People float into the auditorium for the first part of the conference,
mostly middle-aged people, like me, and most with a touch of the
unusual in their dress: a turban, piles of African bracelets, a long

mint-colored scarf. I'm wearing a long multicolored duster, and I suppose when I dressed this morning I had this kind of audience in mind. Among the university leaders more sober suits are the norm; the school aims to teach both transcendental meditation and business success.

I get myself seated in the press section and find a MUM faculty member named Christy Kleinschnitz, who wears a suit of some bright nursery color, and teaches Sanskrit literature. She has the preternatural calm I have been expecting to find here at MUM, from people who meditate at least twice a day. She talks the way the Iowa River flows, with a bare movement.

"We're not creating peace here from the surface level, but from a deeper place," she tells me. She's very earnest. She gives me the first of many talks today I'll get on the Unified Field. In physics the *Unified Field* (a term first used by Einstein) refers to the attempt to create a unified theory of how the smallest particles and most fundamental forces work. When Maharishi followers use the term, they mean a force unifying all of nature and consciousness, uncovered through the use of Superstring Theory. Or I think this is how they use the term.

Christy says, "It's the humming or the reverberation of consciousness interacting with itself because the Unified Field has only itself to interact with. It's the knower and the known and the process of knowing, a tremendous interaction, silence and dynamism that's the source of the manifest universe."

I tell her that's very poetic and she tells me it's a beautiful thing to feel.

The panelists take their seats on the dais: Samite, a musician and political refugee from Uganda; film director David Lynch, who's one of the reasons I wanted to come; a recent graduate of MUM named Erin, who organized the conference; John Hagelin and Sue McGregor, both of whom have MUM affiliations; Robert Muller, former assistant secretary-general of the United Nations; and a member of Physicians for Social Responsibility (PSR) named Maureen McCue. The panelists answer a question about how they would talk to world leaders about creating peace without war, then take questions, then just talk.

The conference addresses peace from different standpoints—inner peace, the Iraq War—but the concept the followers of the Maharishi promote is the idea that if the square root of one percent of any population practices transcendental meditation and yogic flying, violence will drop or end. Even war. Lynch and Hagelin are trying to raise the money to enact this activity on a worldwide scale, building Peace Palaces in major cities and supporting skilled meditators who would then sit in meditation and fly. Hagelin and other Maharishi affiliates have elaborate reasons why this plan will work, having to do with brainwave coherence and the way it will affect the Unified Field. I can't wait to hear Lynch: he seems so odd a person to be touting peace, with his films full of violence, decapitations; a man whose hand's shot off grovels in his own blood to find it, only to have a dog trot it away.

Hagelin, a Harvard-trained physicist, has created an Institute of World Peace, which he directs, and a U.S. Peace Government ("a complementary government" to the present government, Hagelin says, "not there to compete"), and has also run for president as the candidate of the Natural Law Party. Featured in the film *What the Bleep Do We Know!?*, Hagelin wears a camel-colored suit and has an aura of manicure running from the lacquered bald spot on his head to his soft fingers. Lynch also has a look: finer skin, a better dye job on his silver hair than most mortals would have. But in his heavy black mortician's suit and hair that swirls up like a soft-serve ice-cream cone, he's more eccentric.

I have to tell you, before I relate some of the more memorable remarks of this conference, that I spent many hours before the conference arguing with people I know about the square-root-of-one-percent theory, whether that practice could lower crime, lower violence, create peace even if the rest of the population thinks it's bull. It appeals to me, maybe without the granny knot that ties it to physics, but as a statement of faith in the value of the mind. We have physicists who put forward the concept of the Mind-First Universe—Freeman Dyson, who said, in his Templeton acceptance speech, "I do not make any clear distinction between mind and God. God is what mind becomes when it has passed beyond the scale of our comprehension." We seem to sense the possibility at least of consciousness fizzing beyond the borders of the skull, like shaken soda. So why couldn't it do something, out there?

The arguments I have with my friends aren't very intelligent ones, so I'll spare you the details. Suffice it to say my friends tend to say things like "You can't change things with your mind," and I tend to give trenchant answers like "Who knows?" The point is that, as they used to say on *The X-Files,* I want to believe.

David Lynch says he would tell world leaders, "Everything I have learned about peace I have learned from His Holiness Maharishi Mahesh Yogi and his Vedic knowledge. Maharishi has a technique to create permanent world peace. It is one-stop shopping and it is real peace on earth."

The speakers here use a lot of mercantile metaphors, like *one-stop shopping*. I wish I could ask Lynch how someone with a head full of such violent imagery could experience, as he says he does, complete inner peace. Without a trip to more than a single store, even.

John Hagelin says modern global unity is set in the human brain, based "on EEG coherence."

When it's time for questions, I ask David Lynch if the dream of a Unified Field gets reflected by the entertainment media. He says, in the course of my questioning, that I can call him David. Immediately I fall in love with him. I love his swirly-cone hair. I could take a lick of it. "Everybody has a hunger for the Unified Field," he says. "Negativity goes. All positive grows." It will develop today that he likes to talk in quippy rhymes.

So he's saying very little to confirm my desire to believe him, not giving any reasons and saying surprisingly little, for a man who appears intelligent. But, I tell myself, he does seem happy. After my bumpy encounter with the receptionist at the Raj, I haven't been disappointed in that regard. People look very happy. The next speaker, Sue McGregor, who teaches peace and conflict studies at Mount Saint Vincent University in Halifax and serves as a Minister in the Interim Earth Government (another one of these complementary governments created to enact Maharishian ideals; I've begun to lose track of them all and never learn how they meet or what they do), positively bubbles from her glass.

Her talk is funny, since it consists of almost entirely imaginary things.

"I wanted to put your chairs in a circle," she says, "but I can't. So imagine your chairs in a circle." Imagine, she says, you can see one another's faces and there's a space in the center of the room. She says she wanted to use overheads but there's no equipment, so she holds up little pictures, says to imagine we have overheads. On the other hand, she uses the word *whole*—as in *become part of the whole*—throughout her talk, but each time she spells it out, so it's "become part of the w-h-o-l-e." Again and again. Apparently she doesn't put complete faith in our imaginations.

I confess I get lost in Sue McGregor's talk, which strings along a series of metaphors: we are to change our lenses, get into a fertile space, step onto the fertile dance floor, bounce ideas off one another, and go into the Lava lamp, where, it seems, the fertile space is. (At this point she holds up a picture of a Lava lamp, which we kind of pretend is an overhead.) "One idea perks up and pops down and becomes part of a new knowledge," she says, and has us all pat one another on the back for all we've done.

A few people wander up to the dais to ask questions after these talks. An elderly man corners Maureen McCue of the PSR and asks her about the mystery of the "spraying of giant aeresol cans" he's been seeing in the sky. She looks exhausted all of a sudden, and a little cross.

"Jet trails," she says.

BRUCE AND JIN AND I have a free lunch consisting of the worst tofu burger I've ever had, and sit around the grounds of MUM, on lawn chairs and on the grass. I notice David Lynch buying a red bead necklace with a peace sign—the cheap kind, that you could string yourself—and getting a student to clasp it around the neck of his stiff mortician's suit. Then we reconvene in one of the golden domes. The domes are enormous and shiny, filled inside with springy pads. You take your shoes off and find a place to sit. Normally these spaces are used to meditate and to fly. Skeptics describe yogic flying as hopping from a cross-legged position. Some Maharishi followers claim to really fly through the air or levitate to the ceiling. Some concede it is hopping but say that hopping somehow concentrates your brain coherence.

John Hagelin speaks with a voice like lotion about the Unified Field. As he builds in a crescendo, his hand lifts, an inch at a time, for emphasis. "The scientific discovery of the essential unity of life will transform us into a unified world," he tells us, with his hand ascending to the level of his tie. "We have technologies of consciousness now."

When David Lynch speaks again, he's brief, and stresses that he wants to back up Hagelin's comments. "I'm here to promote the Maharishi Mahesh Yogi's peace-creating groups," he says, referring to the Peace Palaces. "Get rid of negativity. It's so simple. We can make a peace-creating factory utilizing the greatest machines on earth—human beings. If we work together we can have real peace on earth this year, heaven on earth this year."

Lynch repeats a few times, "Water the root and enjoy the fruit."

That's it. There's some singing, and everyone leaves the stage without the promised demonstration of yogic flying. No one says anything about the yogic flying, though organizers were talking up the demonstration earlier in the day, and it's been on the website for the conference. I whisper to the people on either side of me: they neither know why the event was canceled nor seem surprised that it was. Finally I ask a local reporter, who asks one of the conference's public relations people, a very slick, groomed guy who has been escorting David Lynch around and managing our press questions. He says they didn't bring the right mats for flying and may do it later.

We leave, at this point, to return to Iowa City.

I want heaven on earth this year. I find myself overwhelmed by a desire to contribute: I can see that peace-creating factory in my head very clearly, like a giant air conditioner blowing out cool, calm air through the power of its human engines.

I HAD ONE ODD MOMENT at the conference. I was once again in the position of asking questions, and I wanted to ask what a paradisical earth would look like, if Maharishi University itself was a microcosm of that peaceful paradise we kept hearing about, with a student body and faculty who had a 100 percent meditation rate, far above the square root of one percent necessary to keep the peace machine humming. In the afternoon session, though, rather than just being allowed to ask questions, we had to tell the slick, curly-headed PR guy what we wanted to ask and he told us rather bossily what to do. I gave him my question and he said, "You have to ask that of Dr. Muller," though Muller wasn't equipped to talk about the school. Dr. Muller's wife answered for him, saying a bit peevishly that I could read all I wanted about Paradise Earth on his website (her pronunciation contained the capital *P* and *E*). Then Muller got to his feet and swept her aside to answer me but still said very little.

Anyway, I was noodling around when I got home, wanting to learn more about Vedic City and the university and David Lynch, when I found after a lot of searching something that might explain their reluctance to tackle my question (to be fair, they may simply have been worried about time). In May of this year a Maharishi University student, Shurvender Sem, pulled a knife in the dining hall and stabbed another student, Levi Butler, to death. Sem stabbed Butler multiple times in the heart without any apparent motive; the two had been friends. Sem had remained unsupervised on campus though earlier that day he had stabbed a student in the face with a pen. Critics, including the uncle of the dead boy, accused the university of burying problems for the sake of its image, so badly do the Maharishi's followers want others to accept the theory of meditation eliminating violence. The school spokesman said the pen incident had seemed minor.

Levi Butler, the victim, was nineteen. The peace conference was dedicated to him, though I noticed this only long after the fact: there's a small dedication in the conference program, and after reading that article from the back issue of a local paper, I went back to the program and recognized his name. The dedication says nothing about how Butler died. It just quotes some of the boy's own writing: "I embrace all things and know they are all valuable. There's no good or bad. There is what is evolutionary and non-evolutionary." And elsewhere: "I am a warrior of God."

SO I SUPPOSE I've been cured of what Bruce would call my romanticism about this belief, recognizing just a bit of my own delusions about crashing motorcycles with my mind. Though I still find them wistfully beautiful, and replay that day often: the silver swirl of hair, like a spirit rising in its optimism; the nursery-colored suit;

even the Lava lamp and the room with its imaginary chairs in a circle and imaginary faces eagerly relating to my imaginary face. I find myself telling people: at least they're trying to do something.

ANYWAY, we're home, back off the main drag of Mormon Trek Boulevard, which seems to be a furious sprawl of construction; there's a new development called The Villages at Mormon Trek, as if the Mormons could have forgotten about Utah and Deseret and simply plunked down here. Silly Mormons. My personal commune and I fall back into routine: do homework, pack the backpack, sing songs to go to sleep. I miss Chris and Olivia and N'Lili and keep up by e-mail and phone. I expect Princess Kay has been taken from her orbit, poured out over corn or stored in someone's freezer or diffused in a kind of grace of toast.

Freeman Dyson said, "God is what mind becomes when it has passed beyond the scale of our comprehension." Well, everything has passed beyond my comprehension now: I don't know why anyone would make a butter sculpture, or why they'd name it Princess Kay, and I don't know where the Mormons went, and I don't know why you could or couldn't fly if you really tried hard enough, and if you did whether that could change the world. I don't know how the pending case of Shurvender Sem will affect things down at the Maharishi University of Management, or if anyone will ever find their Unified Field.

Maybe it's a movement of the spirit, a grace of Fried Twinkies and butter and cross-legged flying, to court incomprehension: to let the mind melt into that Godness of pure confusion. My gating mechanisms, never good, crash around me: everything's flood-

ing in. But I dedicate this moment to grace: I seem to be court-
ing what can pass the scale of my understanding, as if giving this
space to God.

It may not be heaven and earth this year, but still: Princess Kay
looks down on us all, enough sweetness for everyone, our very
own Unified Field. I keep forgetting to tell you: how underneath
it all and through it all, I am so singingly content. *I'm happier than
I've ever been,* N'Lili said. In the sounds of breathing, in the moments edging the return to sleep.

ACCIDENTALS

THE EASTER after the murder, a new preacher comes to campus, one I've never seen before, different from our regulars, like Bible Tom. We get hard men. Loggers, bikers who've found religion. This one blew up from the south on some strange wind. An *accidental,* as bird-watchers call them, dapper in a brown reddish-tinted suit with a striped tie. He wears his hair oiled and even from here, in my office, I see soft fat fingers holding a pointless microphone—pointless because it keeps slipping from his mouth and his voice maintains the same bellow, a preacher's scat that slides from a falsetto to a basso profundo with no intake of breath: "Why is it the song of the *twentieth century* is 'I Can't Get No Satisfaction'? 'I CAN'T GET NO SA-A-A-A-A-TISFACTION!'" On the drawn-out "satisfaction" he lunges forward in a preacher dip.

The twentieth century, he tells us, shook off God and filled us with a void where satisfaction used to be. Of course he's saying this in the twenty-first century, which presumably feels the same.

"JESUS," he tells us, "is the ANSsssssswer."

"What's the question?" someone yells, and the students gathered around him snicker listlessly: it's all boringly scripted.

Behind the preacher stands a boy of perhaps twenty, a student, wearing skimpy white briefs and socks and holding up a white sign that reads

THIS MAN GAVE ME A REALLY GREAT BLOW JOB

The sign is huge. The boy in his thick glasses (that must obscure things in this rain) moves as the preacher moves, standing virtually naked for three hours in the cold March drizzle, grim and purposeful, like someone with a job to do. His blank face looks like a burlesque of the preacher's manic facial mobility. Our preacher, our accidental, hoots; he snarls; he freezes, raptured by his own hallelujahs.

For three hours, when I'm supposed to be writing, I stare out the window, at this passion play between the well-clad faithful man who swoops between the depths and the heights of feeling—always seeming to end on the heights—and the stoic suffering unbeliever. When they leave, they leave; there's a charged empty space, like a pause between sentences.

WHEN TWO of my old dogs died and we flew to Georgia afterward, Jin pressed his head against the window of the plane and called *Burley! Lummi!* over and over. Clouds were smearing along our window, traces of blue beyond. He believed the dogs lived out there, galloping along; this was his idea of heaven. We had told him something similar, I guess, the best we could do at the time. Even now, as I look out the office window at the strips of blue in the sky, it's a color that seems ready to *talk*, though I know it's a color created by the human eye and brain, a shaping of meaningless data, and that fact, too, makes a curlicue of wonder.

"IS THE ANSWER IS THE ANSWER," the preacher said. "Are you a mess, or a message?"

God sees us, he said: our emptiness.

THE GREATEST QUESTION of all is "Why is there something rather than nothing?" I open my e-mail to this one day, in a message perched between others with subjects like TODAY! VITAL TO YOUR DESTINY and LOSE WEIGHT, EAT ALL. (I can shrink my body no matter what I eat. Yeah, it's called dying, I tell the screen.) The latter two I delete.

The first message comes from philosopher Todd Moody, and I read it.

Some modern cosmologists, like Stephen Hawking and Alan Guth, try to show how the laws of nature allow for the spontaneous emergence of something from nothing, in a quantum "burp." But it is odd, to say the least, to claim that the laws of nature existed before nature existed. What were they laws *of*? And if they did exist before nature existed, what manner of existence is that? What does it mean to say that laws can *cause* a universe to appear? I think these laws are being used in these arguments as a surrogate for something that sounds to me very mind-like. So, at the very minimum, I read the Hawking-Guth approach to cosmology as invoking a mind-like cause of nature itself.

(One time a nothing existed and it bubbled with rules. We can look into it, because it's nothing and can be here as easily as there: in its yawning emptiness are laws about quarks and leptons, about electrons fusing like manic hula hoops to nuclei, about cancers that look like weatherbeaten rocks on soft livers and yarns of DNA and seeds flying on tiny parachutes of floss.

Something shakes it out, like a tablecloth primed for the changing courses of a long meal.)

It's a question, Moody tells me, of a Mind-First versus a Matter-First universe, a universe in which laws preexisted matter like a big mind dreaming it out, a Vishnu universe, or one in which the explosion of matter made its own rules. Todd Moody is an agnostic, he says, "at best," though he's the author of a book called *Does God Exist?: A Dialogue.*

I suppose God failed to fill in his? her? its? portion of the text.

I HAVE ALWAYS BEEN RELIGIOUS, even as a child, a very bipolar child. I made notes in my daily diaries about saying prayers and even mentioned praying in my druggy teen years, once writing that I'd prayed that night and felt a real "connection" to the holy, adding, "That was outtasite! Thank you, God!" and moving on to some drug or boy topic. It's typical or stereotypical of manic-depressives to have religious feelings and visions—to the point that both are common message-board subjects—and I'm kind of embarrassed to mention these two sides of my wiring in the same typographic breath. (The relationship between brain activity and religious feeling in all human brains has been explored a lot lately, notably in *Why God Won't Go Away,* by Newburg, D'Aquili, and Rause.) Religion's associated with mania, though I'm just as religious as a depressed person; I merely assume God's gotten sick of me then.

On a Web discussion about whether manic-depressives have a spiritual calling, someone writes,

> In regards to the calling matter, I think of it more as those with bipolar which grants them a certain set of abilities which can be used to help and/or better humankind, then yes, they've a calling; whether that calling is "spiritual" or simply an obligation of honor and morality is beside the point in my opinion.

> There are many people who break the "average" and/or "standard" mold, as they are thought of as "gifted"; so, since our bipolarity may give us abilities which a standard mind lacks, why are we so different from these "gifted" individuals? If I had to wager a guess - I'd say it's due to bipolarity being difficult for a standard person to comprehend; and, people fear what they do not understand.

My priest says, in a sermon, that bipolars and schizophrenics have provided "some of our best prophets." Schizophrenia is known for its linguistic qualities—its streams of neologisms or new words, punning, verbal connections. New ways of looking at the Christian *Logos,* the word. Maybe the lack of mental gatedness, the ability to take in so much outside stimuli all at once, allows some tender connective tissue to emerge, a sense of fingering where the mountains drown and the Western hemlocks point the way of the wind.

Things like the plague of Stendhals happen to me all the time. I don't presume to say it's not coincidence: I've passed the age of knowing. I will say the ungated world's a flood of the dead, the strange, the interesting.

My friend Dawn goes to Mass every Thursday morning at an Episcopal church, though she is not Episcopalian. She prays the rosary, she tells me: matter to atoms to nothingness. She dissolves the tasteless, near-Styrofoam communion wafer on her tongue.

One day I saw myself as a communion wafer, she says once, and the universe took me and dissolved me, and I knew that that was death.

FOR A LONG TIME my tiny church met in a funeral home named—very improbably—Mole's. Icons screened the front of the chapel where we moseyed to take communion: dark-skinned Madonnas with eyes like beaded teardrops holding up grim babes. Next door, in the mortician's office, lay baskets of children's books and blue pamphlets ("It's Not Bad to Be Sad") on dealing with grief.

Here we are, Mole's communicants. Somewhere below us we know bodies lie drained or draining of their fluids, their bloods and milks and lymphs, filling with formaldehyde, the chemical that

might otherwise go into solvents to clean paintbrushes or machines. When they rise at the Day of Judgment, as the dapper
man on my campus tells us—human bodies scrabbling like crabs
from the grave—they will be heavy. They will slosh their way,
smelling like mechanics' rags, to the Judgment Seat.

In spite of our housing we're an oddly cheerful group—all fifteen of us, children squirming and stretching for candles and keys;
adults, afterward, giggling.

That was nice, we say. Let's get breakfast.

Or someone brings a crumb cake, a tray of eggs. As if a
gang of the dead—light, unanchored yet with dying's baptismal
fluids—had arisen and decided to play together at their resting place.

IF WE LIVE in a Mind-First universe, one argument runs, our own
minds exist as microcosms of the creator, little worlds made cun-
ningly indeed. Look at the minds around you and take your pick:
God as Mother Teresa, as the prophet, as the man-in-the-street who
can't remember the latest president's name. As one of the people
in my living room after our dinner party, writing numbers on surface after surface, creating governments (as me burning). Or as all
of us: and if we look at the species swooning at our feet we can see
God—i.e., us—as a cosmic wrecking ball. Which is possible: who
wants what they build to last? No one, if we're any indication. I see
a little boy, gravely bent, create a world out of Lincoln Logs and
wooden train tracks, then sweep it apart with his feet.

Daniel Dennett, a consciousness theorist, famously said that
scholars are a library's way of making another library. Meaning,

we're not the point of this game. God may see us as the whales see us, jittery, complicated and too nervous to live.

IN MY GRADUATE SCHOOL, a student said, "I'll never read a poem with the word *God* in it." He was a gaunt, cynical man who seemed to drink too much, or maybe I just recall him this way because the comment was addressed to me. Someone else in the class added, "or *death*." I went home and pouted about the gaunt cynicism and the drinking and missed the correctness of his position: I'm wasting my time here. Why write the unwritable? Might as well pour the rubber bullets out of your gun and show them around. How can you write death, until you put the pen into your body and draw out its sentences, maybe from the heart that is you and will one day take control of you and punctuate your story; from the brain that electrochemically sends your mind everywhere but to itself.

Albert Einstein, on his deathbed, declared the only one real question to be, Is the universe friendly? Then he turned over and died. Even if we assume the universe is Mind-First, and the mind has something we would think of as consciousness, that tells us nothing about the mind's compassion, how its feet sweep across our particular moment. Whether God's the dapper accidental who condemns us, or the near-naked one, who mocks the notion of condemning and plants the shivering human body behind it all.

THE IDEA of a Matter-First universe, with no underpinning of the metaphysical, is more popular and comes with a high pedigree,

Stephen Hawking and all. Though no matter how much we try to diminish the invisible part of our lives, the nonbodily, we honor it by our fear of what any vacancy in matter might suggest. It shadows us with its simple signs, and we respond by turning away our faces.

We bury. We have always buried. Even before Homo sapiens sapiens or Neanderthals. Around the millennium this discovery shocked archaeologists—a burial pit in northern Spain, 350,000 years old, complete with quartzite ax, a grave good, a gesture to the neediness of death. We in my church hear our sermons about life with lacquered boxes and lacquered bodies in the next room. And children bury; long before the age when developmental psychology tells us they get what death is—its permanent stop—they put birds and bugs in the ground under trowels of earth, with flowers on top, dandelions maybe, a trumpet of azalea. Nothing fancy. Just enough to say something went on here that the earth itself must remark, though we don't care to see the primary evidence.

And one of the five stages of grief is anger. We believe the dead have a choice, not in whether to go but whether to stay gone.

A GRANDFATHER of mine—not the nervous one—was an atheist, the most angry and staunch atheist I have ever known. He was a depressed man, at the very least, with that magma of anger under it. Any religious utterance could drive him to a fury. When missionaries of whatever homegrown faith came to his house with their dark suits and magazines, he yelled and slammed the door. He had fought in World War I and known too many of the dead, my family said, and their habit of interminable exits. His wife, my formidable grandmother, was a Christian Scientist devout in her way, which meant in every way that didn't involve giving up her habit of drinking wine. When this grandfather died, my grandmother sent him off with a big Christian Scientist funeral, violating his wishes and those of his children.

Looking out the window, I think how he would have appreciated the position of the boy in his shorts, even the smutty joke, though the boy in his simple underwear resembled a painting of Jesus on the cross—his arms out at his sides—with the dapper preacher much more like a moneylender at the temple.

BRUCE AND I were once driving through some long stretch of the South—I forget when or why—switching the radio when a voice boomed out, "My Lord ain't no stuck-up man! He's a pal of mine!" That was it. Static crackled in. We picked up then, I think, some Top 40 station and listened to songs about the usual lips and betrayals, whatever folks the singers desired. It comes back to me, that pal of a God, the kind who'd drop a casserole off at your house if you ached with the flu. Especially since my God has been so pummeled with modern science, so bound with those inexhaustible layers of geologic and evolutionary time, that it has no shape at all anymore, and may be nothing now but the layers. Where this man had a face in front of him—a hard face, I imagine, given his own rasp, like our Bible Tom's—and a godly ear cocked to his voice, his troubles, listening.

"More physicists now believe in God than theologians," my priest tells us.

Do I believe in God anymore? I may be closer to the boy in his briefs, freezing, than the fiery preacher. My grandfather, whose sullen moods, whiskey, and powdery oldness always scared me, may be creeping into my face.

That Mind's no pal of mine anymore.

WHAT HAS QUASHED my spiritual sense, at least for the moment—makes me stare at that boy and not the man he shadows—has nothing to do directly with depression or that kind of mood swing but with something else entirely, something that lies deeper than the words of the pair outside my window. My preacher, my accidental, will pass on with his yearly migration. If God Him or Herself came through the Pacific Northwest this way, as a blip timed to a weather or a day, it would seem only appropriate, with our Canada geese, ducks, terns, Steller's sea lions, trumpeter swans, and blizzard of snow geese keeping their annual appointments and leaving. What I do at my desk feels stuck. Not just staying here. Trying to stick the pen in my body and write what doesn't want to be written, God and death and the strangeness of the mind. And love, too, and even things like making dinner and setting up play dates, troweling pansies into my small yard and frowning as they die. The richness of a life I know many people would regard as unstable and diminished, different.

BRUCE, perhaps I'm just writing you a love poem now: the best I can do. I've been settling for that a lot lately. And Jin. Because of this illusion I have that you both live in my body, that we're together, in some real way, when all along your hearts beat in your own chests, pumping out your time, and that is something I can't touch. We lie in bed; you've been reading Rupert Sheldrake and thinking about morphic fields, the webbing Sheldrake sees passing over the world, connecting minds. Yesterday I saw a picture of a beast in my head, then you mentioned the city named after it, Buffalo. We do this kind of thing all the time, tie up the phone calling each other at once, suddenly begin talking about the etymology of "night." One night, if you remember, we woke up having dreamed the same elaborate dream. We dreamed of the death of a mother and found out later a friend's mother was dying.

Let's see if we can read each other's minds, you say.

You say, I'm thinking of a color.

I do see a stripe of velvet color in my mind, in front, almost, of my thinking, which is trying to find a way out of your experiment. I don't want to know we can't do this; I don't want to know we can. Blue.

Blue. That's it. Try a number from one to ten.

Five.

Five.

We're silent for a while. We have begun to live in two places, one close but even more darkly foreign then ourselves, with a heart and mind more traitorous and distinct. Stalking suddenly into the kitchen for an apple.

You say, a number from one to one hundred.

That's ridiculous.

Please.

For another minute we concentrate, sending something along that sticky, soft line.

Ninety-eight.

I was thinking ninety-nine.

I don't want to do this anymore, it's giving me the creeps, so I say so and flop over on my side, burying myself in covers. My cat climbs on me. I tuck the pillow under my head, wanting to drift off and not think.

I'VE ALWAYS BELIEVED in God. Maybe I'm just trying to avoid thinking of losing my place in the web, whether as a fly wrapped up in an alien cocoon or the orb spider, who both, for different reasons, twang the silks. Maybe consciousness is no more meaningful to the universe than a rhyzomatic plant, sending its runners out looking for new places to root. A strawberry, a mint, easily weeded. Bruce's uncle tells us of our church, "You just want this to be true. That's all anybody can say, who's selling that soap." Because we fear death but crave sleep.

Is the universe friendly. Burley! Lummi! It's so naked, that look out the airplane window: that *I want to see you again.*

MY MIND WAYS give me an inability to see things simply. So I stop and stare, the way my depressed grandfather used to; I stare, thinking of the crystalline chains of molecules making up my desk. When I was a child, my world had edges; my cat let me know whether God was pleased with me; the sharp grasses at the Jersey shore told me to go away, in spaces now filled in and covered with tract housing. Things could press so hard I plotted my death with extra-strength Excedrin or swallowed little moons of Quaaludes; now I don't do that, but each fall, when the light decreases, I experience it as a living burial; I feel shovelfuls of dirt on my skin. I still become entirely lost, staring at the tangerine color of a book, the shiny nubbing of the white wall. Maybe it's a hospital's way of making more hospitals, a psychoactive drug's way of creating hosts. Or my tribe consists of meme machines, puffing out new air. ("Mental representations, or memes, transform the space in which they evolve.") Spilling out religion in prophecy, and roiling color. Simply paying attention to the dead. One of Darwin's central points was that, to be robust and successful, a species needs to remain as diverse as possible, allowing for millions of possible reactions to evolutionary pressures. We humans could conceivably genetically engineer ourselves to oblivion.

I HAVE A CAT. I use the phrase out of habit, because at this point *having* has nothing to do with it. She sits with me and walks with me and when she's lying on me there's no more weight than the feeling of your fist in your lap. My cat, Savannah, has black and white markings, common alley cat: a black patch on her nose, black tail, spatterwork through the rest. When she opens her mouth to yawn she shows another world of markings, dark and light worked in rounds on her upper palate, a microcosm of her body. She is a little cosmos of fine blueprints.

"It seems to point to an intelligence," my computer says,
"that does the fine-tuning"
FAITH MAY COME TO YOUR AID
DESTINY!

We are all following the preacher, with our white signs.

I WRITE to Bill Calvin and ask him if he believes in God, or anything like a God.

When I drive down to Seattle to talk to Calvin, he describes
a world, maybe already happening, of different kinds of humans
forming—*speciating*—who cannot mate. He talks about a county
in California with polluted water and a very high miscarriage
rate, in which children who are born could develop enough
unique characteristics that they could only mate with one another. Forming separate humans, the gorillas and orangutans and
chimps of the human world. This he can see. My God question
he never answers.

My head is aching with big questions. I go to my forebear
Christopher Smart, manic-depressive poet from the eighteenth
century. Confined to a madhouse, with the whips and ropes of the
period and every reason for misery, he wrote one of the most ecstatic poems ever, *Jubilate Agno,* a religious celebration a large
chunk of which focused on his alley cat, Jeoffry. Oddly enough
Smart, in his religious ecstasies, loving the world if only because
it contained the one glory of his cat, was a close friend of Samuel
Johnson's, the man who expected the sane to go mad if they

thought too deeply about their lives. "My poor friend Smart," Johnson liked to say.

> *For I will consider my Cat Jeoffry.*
> *For he is the servant of the Living God, duly and daily*
> *serving him.*
> *For at the first glance of the glory of God in the East he*
> *worships in his way.*
> *For this is done by wreathing his body seven times round with*
> *elegant quickness.*
> *For then he leaps up to catch the musk, which is the blessing of*
> *God upon his prayer.*
> *For he rolls upon prank to work it in.*
> *For having done duty and received blessing he begins to*
> *consider himself.*
> *For this he performs in ten degrees.*
> *For first he looks upon his forepaws to see if they are clean.*
> *For secondly he kicks up behind to clear away there.*
> *For thirdly he works it upon stretch with the forepaws extended.*
> *For fourthly he sharpens his paws by wood.*
> *For fifthly he washes himself.*
> *For sixthly he rolls upon wash.*
> *For seventhly he fleas himself, that he may not be interrupted*
> *upon the beat.*

Instead of all the other things I could think about I think about Savannah, who has passed her twenty-first birthday (Ancient of Days, we call her). I don't think she gives me special messages, but I do love her beyond all reason; I think about her all day long.

How I once scraped her, a lump, from under pieces of furniture and plastered her down on my lap. It took time but she got greedy for touch. Soon she'd purr for me when I scratched the velvet right behind her ears, adding long sweeping strokes along her backbone, thumb and forefinger winged apart. I hauled her onto my lap, and once she got used to the idea that we were together, like it or not, I began my stroking and she learned to purr, as it turned out, with no shyness or dignity at all. When she purrs, she points her nose up at me and languidly blinks her eyes shut and open.

For eighthly he rubs himself against a post.
For ninthly he looks up for his instructions.

After a few weeks in my Brooklyn apartment she started to scrabble onto my lap herself, to seek out that near-annihilating touch. Soon she started sleeping on me and has for the double decade since, on chest if I sleep on my back, on butt if my stomach. When she's awake, she follows me around the house. I fold laundry, I pick up toys, I throw things into a pot on the stove for stock. She shadows my secular movements, holy fool.

After we had experienced each other for a while, Savannah would climb into my lap and begin purring no matter what I did. Now I can ignore her, I can roll over and shove her off in my sleep (which I do several times a night); sometimes I get irritated and say, "Jeez, what makes·you think I can just *stop* right now, Savannah?," for instance when I'm trying to work at the computer and getting nowhere and she makes her way to me by stomping along the computer keys. Still I wake several times a night to the sound of her grinding approval and the eyes opening and closing in the dusky light.

Because I learned over time that I had to do less and less, that my existence became its own offering. Like when I wake up in the middle of the night and the bodily heft of my husband and son, the mist of their being, gives me license to sleep again. After some years—ten maybe?—if she came into the room where I stood opening the mail or something, she'd crouch down and purr. She's not really shy anymore: my son carries her around the house, like a rag dangling; she's six pounds and we work to keep the weight on. She's living backbone, a set of vertebrae knuckled and dominating her back. Her stomach hangs straight down. She's not the soft, shy thing she was; she's not the same Savannah. Except she is.

One day I'm sorting laundry in our small living room and I notice it, the little engine of pleasure starting, and I know she's there somewhere, probably under the woodstove looking at me, and I'm irritated and busy and the clothes have ink stains on them again and I'm not going to stop and pet her, but even if she knew that, it wouldn't make any difference. I'm here, and the hands that could descend if they chose. In relation to the world, this could be all we're heading for, quieting down to know that it's there and can touch us in a particular way. Perhaps we can always exist like this, as the body and not the body quite. This is what we can hope for in the end *(Poor Jeoffry! poor Jeoffry! the rat has bit thy throat)*. This is death maybe.

LANGUAGE GARDEN

The very concept of a present moment is only
meaningful to one who is trapped in time by
being conscious.

—CONSCIOUSNESS THEORIST JARON LANIER

Were you to live 3,000 years, or even 30,000,
remember that the sole life which a man can lose is
that which he is living at the moment; and
furthermore, that he can have no other life except the
one he loses. This means that the longest life and the
shortest amount to the same thing. For the sole thing
of which any man can be deprived is the present, since
this is all he owns, and nobody can lose what is not his.

—MARCUS AURELIUS, *Meditations*

I LIVE IN A LANGUAGE GARDEN. When I moved in here,
to my small house in Bellingham, I decided in one of my manic-
obsessive fits to plant every plant I'd ever seen mentioned in a
Shakespeare play. This meant, because I have something of a pho-
tographic memory (a manic gift), lying awake at night reading off
fragments of the plays in my head—on the page (smudged and
creased if it was) and in the typeface I'd first encountered them.
I drove to Seattle for wormwood and rue; I didn't tell anyone what
I was doing but regarded my garden as a kind of conjure, a sphere

of magical protection, a planting of voices (there's fennel for you, and columbine). Shakespeare's plants, sprung from the mind of a dead man, felt more lasting than the always bolting, drooping, jaundicing things outside my window. (I'll give violets away; they withered all when my father died.) What I could not find in Shakespeare I planted for the name: let the delphiniums die but nurtured the toadflax, spread the lambs' ears, mulched the veronica with precious dung. As if I could turn matter into words.

My yard now blooms with unintentional comedy: the balm wants to overtake and bury the rue, and I weed and weed it back; the wormwood died, not liking my soil's particular brand of gall. The rue returns every year from a gnarled stump the size of a large sweet potato, bleached and dead-looking, and when the tiny sprouts emerge, it's so improbable I expect them to grow into something else, something less rueful. Fennel, that licorice of untruth, wants like the prolific balm to take over the garden.

I HAVE BEEN READING a great deal about animal minds lately, talking about them to Dawn during our afternoons at Stuart's and at our houses. It feels like a question, an obscure question Dawn with her Asperger's has had at least partly answered working with gorillas. Wondering what an ape might teach me about the mind ways of myself and the people in my world, I get an introduction from Dawn, and fly to see and speak with an orangutan named Chantek.

Chantek lives in a habitat on the grounds of Grant Park Zoo in Atlanta, where he was placed after a stint at Yerkes Primate Center, and before that, outgrowing the home of his "cross foster-mother," as anthropologist Lyn Miles calls herself. She raised him as a signing infant from the age of nine months, rearing him as much as possible like a human child. Lyn toilet-trained Chantek and gave him chores, like cleaning his room, and an allowance. (His favorite thing to spend it on is fast food from McDonald's, though his weight has ballooned to obese levels. If he's granted legal rights, as Lyn would like him to be, he could join the fast-food class-action lawsuit and become not just the most verbal but the richest orang in the world. But in the interests of Chantek's heart, no McDonald's for now.)

When our van pulls up to Chantek's habitat he swings out onto one of its inside branches and asks for bottled water, which he calls "car water," since Lyn usually has some in her car. He's particular about bottled waters, preferring Naya, but he'll settle for this, Dasani. Chantek appears harmlessly shaggy as a Sesame Street figure, the pumpkin color of seventies carpet, the size of an enormous easy chair. Because of his strength, though, we're not allowed into his habitat, so he kisses and strokes Lyn through the bars.

I know very little sign, so Lyn asks Chantek to teach me a little. Chantek has an active vocabulary of about three hundred words and a passive vocabulary of a thousand or more, which he can comprehend either by speech or by sign. We start with the basics.

Teach her apple, says Lyn.

Chantek shows me apple, brushing his cheek. I mimic him and Good, he says, then asks Lyn what's wrong with her hand, which has a scratch on the knuckle.

I did it cleaning, she tells him, and he makes a grimace of sympathy, then asks to touch and kiss it.

Lyn introduces me as Writer—which becomes my sign name—the friend of Dawn You Made a Necklace For. Chantek has had surgery recently on his laryngeal flap, the long black fold under the chin that makes orangs look like some kind of colonial barrister, and she asks him how he's feeling, if the suture's healing okay. Yes, says Chantek, he's fine. He has missed Lyn and wants to play ball. Oh, and there's poop on the other side of the habitat, presumably left there by his companion, Sibu; it's dirty and he'd like it removed.

Lyn and Chantek speak head to head; her disorderly reddish hair makes them look for a second like mother and son, a shorn and repetitious mother, a leaning son anxious not to misunderstand. I stand around like anyone hanging around two family members who chat familiarly, neither of whom you know very well; you try to find ways to interject yourself into the conversation (mine turns out to be no more mysterious than a bag of yellow raisins, which Chantek loves but Jin got tired of). In other words, with one part of my mind I'm aware of the fact that I'm doing this slightly unreal thing, talking with an orangutan. With another, I'm just a socially awkward person in a group, hoping I don't say anything stupid, and that I can perhaps say or do something a little memorable.

"Sad," Chantek says when we, or more precisely, Lyn, leaves.

CHANTEK USES WORDS plus gestures to speak: he might tell Lyn "I you talk," indicating the other side of the cage, when he wants privacy from me—from my keen and almost predatory listening—as he does several times when I'm there. (He insists on privacy to discuss the feces he wants cleaned up.) His inability or unwillingness to use complicated syntax puts him at a child's linguistic level, as do other behaviors—in some ways his resemblance to Jin and every other human child in the world cracks me up. When we give him an apple and ask him to share it with his habitat-mate, Sibu, he carefully pulls off a crumb of apple flesh and hands it to her. ("Really share or you can't have any more," Lyn scolds orally, and he resignedly breaks off half.) He signs over and over—begs—for ice cream and cheeseburgers. Other things I see show a sophistication a child wouldn't have—Chantek, as always, dabs his mouth clean after eating but surprises us by folding the napkin to a fresh side and sponging out the sutured part of his laryngeal flap, an area that tends to catch food crumbs. He has never cleaned this area in the past and seems to realize the suture needs special attention. Sibu, an orang that has never had human acculturation, grabs a napkin and begins wiping her mouth as she watches his slow and deliberate swipes. It's not quite the apes throwing bones in the air in front of a monolith from the film *2001,* but Sibu has clearly, at that moment, absorbed a piece of culture.

AFTER VISITING WITH CHANTEK, Lyn and I drive to the zoo's McDonald's to talk for a while. I've jotted down a few questions to ask, and Lyn responds by diagramming Chantek's intelligence: she ranks him at about human age five to eight in mental development, with a striking skill for art (Jane Goodall called his artistic work "the most remarkable thing she ever saw an ape do").

"And that makes sense," Lyn tells me. "Orangs spend most of their time foraging in dense jungle. They're very visual." It makes me wonder if a piece of Chantek's mind might feel bipolar—his paintings show wild, exuberant swirls of color.

Lyn tells me how she sees Chantek's mind, grabbing a thin napkin and drawing on it, her Chantek-hair bent forward. She draws Chantek's mind as three circles and an oval, a wedge of each circle overlapping the oval at the base. One piece of Chantek remains the ape mind as it's existed in the wild, one resembles normal human intelligence, one neuroatypical human—an autistic might share Chantek's visual sense of the world; Chantek's color processing might resemble mine. The long oval that juts far from the rest covers pieces of the other circles but represents something new: enculturated ape. Apes who will put at least some experiences into words; who will look to their world to provide glitters and shapes and colors for their art, who will have an aesthetic we can only start to admire, as we admire the navigational abilities of a blind man crossing the street.

A project called Ape Net is working to put video feeds into Chantek's cage, to enable him to talk to Koko, a gorilla in California who also signs—an interspecies chat undertaken in terms of human language but not directed by humans.

"We want to find out what challenges them, what gives their life meaning," says Lyn. It occurs to me that we have no protocol that answers these questions about ourselves. Maybe we are, like the proverbial screwballs who go into the field of psychiatry, posing the questions we would like to force ourselves to answer.

AS MARCUS AURELIUS REMINDS US, whatever meaning we find in the world must be crammed into a mighty short space. Most would agree it's a small world (our present lasts about two to fifteen seconds, according to Merlin Donald and other consciousness theorists), elegantly borne on the litter of a body that's mostly 4-billion-year-old water. We're the ultimate May-December marriage.

THE TERM *PERSONHOOD* gets used a lot in the field of animal intelligence. The website Lyn set up for Chantek proclaims him the "World's First Orangutan Person and Ambassador for the Rainforest" over a head shot of him, looking solemn and ambassadorial. Personhood means language, self-awareness, socialization to such a degree that rights would have to be conferred under the law. We value personhood; it meant a lot to the family of Tommy Munsen to use the lower-case, to strip personhood from Kyle Anderson. How animals might see us, who fast-forward them, or subvert them, with our system of mental coding, I wonder about: as those mythical small gods, like Hermes or Prometheus, who always annoy the hell out of the great gods, or as a defect given to them, an interspecies virus maybe, "a disease that's in my blood," as Lear said, "that I must needs call mine." We may build in them the world of neurotypicals and atypicals.

Language, I remind myself watching Chantek, forms one cognitive tool among many, and possibly a weak one. We can't know. What Lyn and her Ape Net cohort imply is that without some humanizing of apes—this ability to see them whine like a human child for a cheeseburger—they will be wiped out by humans unable to put a mental face to them. Though I imagine an ape-raised human, tested in the intelligences that keep orangs going in their world, like the ability to read body stance and facial expression—asked to judge, for instance, an array of smiles. To display the visual and tracking skills to find lychees and mandarins tucked into the dense jungles of Indonesia. We would seem childlike, very dim.

LYN WANTS CHANTEK to have freedom. He grew up in her trailer on the campus at the University of Tennessee at Chattanooga, and escaped from his living quarters looking for food. When Chantek was eight, the university shipped him back to Yerkes, his birth facility, which allowed Lyn limited visits for a few years, then declined her the right to see Chantek altogether.

"They said they wanted to put the animal back into him," she tells me. Lyn says this with some bitterness and I don't push it, though looking at my notebook later I wonder what it means, since Yerkes pioneered primate language; would an ape troubled by his own shit be too much? Lyn finally regained control of Chantek and had him placed at the zoo, moving to Atlanta to stay close. Chantek is not part of any zoo exhibit—he lives a short ride off from the main zoo grounds—and while he has a roomy habitat with plenty of branches for swinging, as well as a hammock and private space, it's still a cage.

When I meet Chantek I stare into his eyes, wondering, wanting to feel a kinship: that he knows me, that I can know him somehow. Orangs are the stillest of the apes; they can swing and swing and then freeze. Buddha-like, Chantek watches me back without expression. I want to say he tells me (Buddha-like), Figure it out for yourself. But he probably sees something as inexplicable as life in me, in my humanness.

Consciousness, most theorists say, is language: what lets you know yourself, know time: self-aware. If you're a Lanierist you can argue that we have given Chantek, in the gift of language, a more terrible prison than the steel one: the jail of the present, with its fine-honed edge. (Now Lyn is here, Chantek hears in his head. Now she leaves.) Or you could argue, with linguist Derek Bickerton ("Only language could have broken through the prison of immediate experience in which every other creature is locked, releasing us into infinite freedoms of space and time"), that with language the doors of Chantek's cage have been flung open in a way no key could ever fling them.

Out of his jungle garden and into mine (here's apple for you, and water; you must wear your rue with a difference).

I READ THAT KOKO the gorilla calls death, in an extraordinary string of thought, "comfortable hole byebye." Before coming here I imagined myself having talks like that with Chantek, finding out what the hole is, what the comfort. But he teaches me a few words and, satisfied by my basic sufficiency, turns to Lyn, occasionally cadging my raisins. Or he sits still and regards me thoughtfully from his pale, fur-curtained eyes.

Flummoxed, I sit on a rock and sing, the only song that comes to mind.

> *Some bright morning when my life is o'er*
> *I'll fly away*

To that home on God's celestial shore
I'll fly away

It's an old slave spiritual, one I have always used to sing Jin to sleep.

MY YARD SWARMS with fruit flies, celebrating their daily birthdays. The flies love my raspberries—unpickable in their plenty at this time of year, so they end up getting that grayish patina of rot, and rucking in on themselves on their canes. Rotting makes the fruit alcohol the flies love and they hang out there in jittering waves, or in my open compost pail, or in my kitchen. Fruit flies are a mandala of nature, living a week—a drunken week—then dying to be swept up by some wind, beautiful and intricate for all that: red eyes not too different from the darkening drupelets of the raspberries, brown wings and a black body.

I'll fly away O glory I'll fly away

CAN I ADMIT to being such a wimp of a writer? I hate to be away from my family. I love them. It flies in the face of what I was taught to consider a right dedication to the creative, romantic spirit. They challenge me and give my life meaning and it's our habit to do most things together. Both have flown with me to Atlanta—I scheduled this visit around some poetry readings of Bruce's; right now he takes Jin through the zoo, seeing the truly caged creatures, while Chantek teaches me a language he knows and I do not. Last time we came here Jin began singing "I'll Fly Away" out of the blue at a Krispy Kreme Doughnuts place, loud, and a heavy middle-aged woman who'd been serving doughnuts dashed from behind the counter, her face suddenly alive.

"No, you got to sing, 'I *believe* I will fly away,'" she told him as she sang too. "You got to sing 'I *know* I will fly away.'"

> O how glad and happy when we meet
> I'll fly away
> No more cold iron shackles on my feet
> I'll fly away

CHANTEK CALLS HIMSELF an "Orangutan Person." Presumably this term would refer to any orang who'd been enculturated and given language. Untaught orangutans, like his cagemate, Sibu, he's given the rather snide name of "orange dog." He sees himself somehow as the ape in the Web photo, stiff, solemn, buttoned-up as a character in *Planet of the Apes.* It sounds exalted as well as lonely: the only one of his kind in the universe, as far as he knows.

THREE CIRCLES and an oval. I wonder what in my circle of alternative thinking might be caught in the wedge Chantek's oval covers—if, for instance, he *feels* any of the multiplicity we record in his intelligence: language here, art there. Given what we know of his mind, it's not hard to imagine there may be a part of him he sees as "Orangutan Person," whom he might visualize clothed, like us, holding a bottle of named water. And a part that remains Orange Dog, warm in its fur, smelling its way through, like the blinded Gloucester in *Lear*.

CHANTEK'S OVAL is an oval because it arcs out into the future. There's no sense yet of what enculturated ape will become, because, as Lyn points out, social groups cocreate themselves and their "personal forms of meaning, in groups and subgroups, much as a family does." Ape Net's goal is to develop 90 acres on Maui—which the group already owns—into a habitat that will allow a separate culture of socialized apes to form. It will take a lot of money and remains an idealistic vision, an ape Eden. You can see, in Koko the gorilla's words, a difference already between us: we tend to imagine going up at the end; she saw down.

Maybe they'll forget it all and choose grunts and touch and grooming over our brand of civilization. Or maybe in a hundred thousand years they'll have their own transit that speeds along the ground and their children will hang out the window, heads down to the lower earth, crying out the names of lost pets.

As I look at Lyn's oval again, I see that elliptic of new ape consciousness as an infinity sign, untwisted. A new mind is evolution, after all, which reeks of time. The oval forms a complement to its cousin the infinity sign—an oval that's been looped or kinked. Aurelius and philosopher Ned Markosian put their money on those things that jam into the present; Merlin Donald wails, "How could a person stitch together a meaningfully conscious existence from an endless series of two- to fifteen-second samples of experience?" Others, like Augustine, deny the reality of anything but the celestial or infinite. Tier of garden knots and wringer-out of far too much laundry, I tend to see how the twisted shape will wriggle to unbend itself, the infinity sign undo.

The future's a world. *To that home on God's celestial shore.* O brave new world, said Miranda.

MY FENNEL-HEART has come through here once. I did not sing to Chantek, except in my mind, looking at his bars, which my imaginings of our encounter had never contained. It shocked me, the ape in a cage (Lear said, *Unaccommodated man is no more but such a poor, bare, forked animal*). Unlike my son, I don't have the chutzpah to sit in front of strangers belting out my melody-induced belief that I'll fly away. I did get flummoxed at Chantek's habitat and sit down on the rocks, and watch him string necklaces out of leather and beads, knotting the spaces between beads with his teeth. His black palms like car leather. I did feel like an idiot.

Why do I lie to you? When the truth's persuasive enough, I think, and occupies this space almost wholly. Chantek, Lyn, my loved family, my funky garden with its nurtured knobs of rue. The lie like a weed in there, or a plant's unwanted corming. Perhaps to even out our relationship: I behind these lines, carrying out my fantastic gestures, you free. It may be about Chantek, or it may not.

I KNOW WHOLE ACTS of Shakespeare's plays by heart, and when I want to enjoy them and not just search for plant references, I have staged many of them in my head when I should have been sleeping. I have actors for each part, and line readings, cos-

tumes, gestures. It hurts, in some ways, to see actual plays per-
formed: directors cut them, the actors look wrong, and I tend not
to like their deliveries. I know how it should be done. "To be or
not to be," for instance, I want as a near-whisper. When a play arrives in my head it comes wholly, as a note of music and a scene
with the players in motion, maybe King Claudius in burgundy
and gold holding a chalice before his lords, and then the words.

Thomas Huxley once tried to describe infinity by saying infinite monkeys with infinite typewriters would eventually produce
the works of Shakespeare. No more interesting than saying that infinite humans with infinite caves and infinite predators would
eventually echolocate like bats (in fact, I expect that would happen a hell of a lot faster). Enough monkeys with enough time will
produce their own version of Shakespeare—maybe have—and it
will have all that uplift and melancholy beauty, and will probably
be dumb to us. It may be a sequence of grunts or leaves chewed
and spat out on a lychee branch. We may stomp it out or cut it
down because we do not see it.

MY CHILD DEVELOPMENT BOOKS tell me children put down
virtually no memory until around four, when they have well-
developed language. Though it's impossible, I would like to visit
Chantek's memory now. It seems very likely he's begun to store
material as language; not just a simple object like a ball (surely a
dog can do that much), but past events, which I imagine he stores
as simple sentences (Mother Lyn hurt finger, Writer visit with
Mother Lyn). Perhaps he sees them again, relives them, the way humans have become so adept at carrying and replaying hurt and

shame. We have *inner critics, depressive realism,* where we narrate our lives to ourselves with deadly precision, as King Lear comes to do (*Is man no more than this?* the king says, and *A dog's obeyed in office . . .*). Chantek's not such a good presentist, such a good Aurelian, anymore. We have given him that quality, of useless repetition, as we've hammered it into ourselves, so that even humans who've devoted their lives to voiding the existence of the past and future live in them regardless.

You need to cut out the negative self-talk, a therapist scolds me. *You need to let go of the past.*

Here the part of me that lies in Chantek's oval may grow. Memory lives in mania, a word-onslaught, not just of Shakespeare plays but twigs and bits of kindergarten gaffes and offerings of Velveeta from young and insecure mothers and husbands you don't know will be husbands casually asking why you don't smoke anymore. It's language roused to a frenzy that devours itself, almost: it's exhilarating but ultimately painful to live your life all at once; it's not the job the Aurelian minute's meant to do. Blah blah blah my mind starts saying after a while. Blah blah blah blah blah blah blah. The brain burning. Not Derek Bickerton's infinite freedom of language but an infinite press of time on the instant. That spark in Chantek's mind we stand in front of with our bellows. Words may mean nothing to Chantek ultimately, or they may mean negative self-talk and depressive realism—*I am a fat ape among apes*—or an asyntactic flood of nonexistent existence.

RIGHT NOW, within the bonds of the present, the neighbor boy's reggae music blasts far too loud and Mars's path has brought it closer to the earth than it's been in 60,000 years, so the Red Planet flames at night over Venus and the moon, usurping the North Star's glow. When it last appeared like this, Neanderthals, the dominant human, looked up at it as I do now, at an eye in the sky like a saber-toothed cat's, gleaming. *ooo-woo. ooo-woo. mer.*

I have taken to being outside all the time, to doing nothing, a statue of myself. Nothing feels as though it has any point. For the moment. But I like to look at the bald eagles here, the black squirrels, the pleats of the pink mallow and the fuchsia, crazy offerings to the gods of the present. And the momentary fruit flies, whose lives and mine are precisely equal. Their few seconds all the wealth that can be taken from me.

If it be so, said Lear, *it is the chance which doth redeem all sorrow / that ever I have felt.*

I don't think I'm a presentist yet. Perhaps only an Aurelian, seeing in language that which dissolves into nothing, in seconds, even if someone tries to make it live again in her garden bed. When we come together—ape and human, author and reader— we settle for demonstrating we both know the grossest objects of the earth, *ball* and *hurt* and *water,* while what we would want to name's fluid and intestinal: the melancholy in the eyes of a caged ape; or a man and a boy, hand in hand at a zoo. We have given Chantek a way of knowing the past, the gift of the void. Of remembering the red star suddenly burning and the dark-haired woman named Writer who looked at him hungrily, and the question she must have left behind in his speaking mind: of what she could possibly want.

NOTES

PROLOGUE

p. 6, *By some estimates*: See U.S. Department of Education annual reports to U.S. Congress, last ten years.

p. 6, *An extensive* Time *magazine article*: "Young and Bipolar," *Time,* August 19, 2002.

p. 7, *For many of us, the difficulty of finding other people*: "I know that certainly for the autistic community the Web has made a huge difference to many because it gives them a social life and a chance to communicate that they otherwise might not have had access to, as well as helping people to find a group identity," writes an autistic correspondent, Suz, who goes on to add, "I want to see the culture, the values, and the language of the autistic community spread beyond the net, even though there is no doubt that without the net they could not have been born."

p. 7, *"Attention Deficit Disorder was coined by regularity chauvinists"*: Ted Nelson, cited in Gary Wolf, "The Curse of Xanadu," *Wired,* June 1995.

p. 7, *"She sends me, one day, an article"*: Speech reported by Newsmax.com, September 13, 2004.

THE HUMAN ROAD

p. 28, *Scientists like the late Donald Griffin*: Donald Griffin, *Animal Minds: Beyond Cognition to Consciousness* (Chicago, IL: University of Chicago Press, 2001.) See also Roger Payne, *Among Whales* (New York: Scribner's, 1996).

I AM THE NAME IT HAD

p. 75, *Paul Collins, father of an autistic son*: Paul Collins, *Not Even Wrong: Adventures in Autism* (London: Bloomsbury, 2004).

SHIP OF FOOLS

p. 94, *Foucault writes*: This and the following comments from Foucault are drawn from Michel Foucault, *Madness and Civilization,* translated by Richard Howard (New York: Vintage Books, 1967).

p. 94, *"mocking laughter and insulting pity"*: The doctor cited is Jean-Étienne-Dominique Esquirol.

p. 101, *I found this Walter Scott quote*: A. Brigham, "Insanity—Illustrated by Histories of Distinguished Men, and by the Writing of Poets and Novelists," *The American Journal of Insanity,* vol. 1, issue 9, 1844. As with Foucault, quotes of his following are drawn from this source.

p. 102, *Johnson, Brigham's hero*: Cited in Brigham, "Insanity."

p. 110, *It's like the question of depressive realism*: D. G. Myers, *Social Psychology* (Toronto: McGraw-Hill, 1999).

p. 110, *A Johns Hopkins psychologist wrote*: Alexander Truskinovsky, M.D. "Literary Psychiatric Observation and Diagnosis Through the Ages: *King Lear* Revisited," *Southern Medical Journal,* vol. 95, issue 3, 2002.

HEARING VOICES

p. 119, *As cognitive neuroscientist Merlin Donald says*: Merlin Donald, *A Mind So Rare: The Evolution of Human Consciousness* (New York: Norton, 2002).

p. 120, *we who are "tribal and aggressively territorial"*: E. O. Wilson, "Is Humanity Suicidal?" *New York Times Magazine*, May 30, 1993.

p. 121, *As anthropologist Ian Tattersall says*: Ian Tattersall, *The Monkey in the Mirror: Essays on the Science of What Makes Us Human* (New York: Harvest Books, 2003).

p. 122, *In fact, you are more likely than anything to be like me*: See Ronald Kessler, U.S. Comorbidity Survey of 1991–1992, and follow-ups.

p. 123, *Bipolars—"restless and unquiet"*: Research in support of this migration theory has been generated by Martin Voracek of the University of Vienna; N. Hunt, Mandy Sharpley, and Gerard Hutchinson in England; and others.

p. 128, *"Perhaps a law of evolution"*: Wilson, "Is Humanity Suicidal?"

p. 130, *As opposed to Neanderthals*: See Ian Tattersall, *Extinct Humans* (Boulder, CO: Westview Press, 2001).

p. 134, *William Calvin details the burst of human language*: Detailed in William H. Calvin, *A Brain for All Seasons: Human Evolution and Abrupt Climate Change* (Chicago: University of Chicago Press, 2003).

p. 137, *Ian Tattersall points out the mistake*: Tattersall, *The Monkey in the Mirror*.

p. 137, *what scientist Julian Huxley calls*: Julian Huxley, *Essays of a Biologist*. (London: Chatto and Windus, 1926).

AMONG THE BEAUTIFUL CROWS

p. 141, *I'm reading an article titled "Creativity, Evolution and Mental Illnesses"*: A. Preti and P. Miotto, "Creativity, Evolution and Mental Illnesses," *Journal of Memetics*, vol. 1, 1997.

p. 141, *I just finished an old article*: N. C. Andreasen and I. D. Glick, "Bipolar Affective Disorder and Creativity: Implications and Clinical Management," *Comprehensive Psychiatry*, vol. 29, 1988.

p. 141, *fewer gating mechanisms for outside stimuli*: The research of Shelley Carson of Harvard and Jordan Peterson of the University of Toronto on latent inhibition also supports this.

p. 143, *Real both philosophically and literally*: Benjamin Libet, "Unconscious Cerebral Initiation and the Role of Conscious Will in Voluntary Action," *Behavioral and Brain Sciences*, vol. 8, 1985.

PANDEMONIUM ON ZOMBIE EARTH

p. 158, *a statement that seems written for this weekend*: Donald, *A Mind So Rare*.

p. 159, *"The speed at which species are being lost"*: Quoted in "Mass Extinction Underway, Majority of Scientists Say," *Washington Post*, April 21, 1998.

p. 159, *I come across this*: Ivan Havel, "Living in Conceivable Worlds,"*Foundations of Science, vol. 3, 1999.

p. 161, *Thomas Metzinger writes something that staggers me*: T. Metzinger, ed., *Conscious Experience* (Exeter, NH: Imprint Academic, 1985).

p. 166, *I'm scratching, and also thinking of cognitive theorists George Lakoff and Mark Johnson*: George Lakoff and Mark Johnson, *Philosophy in the Flesh: The Embodied Mind and Its Challenge to Western Thought* (New York: Harper-Collins, 1999).

p. 166, *This cognitive model*: Oliver Selfridge, "Pandemonium: A Paradigm for Learning," in *Symposium on the Mechanization of Thought Processes* (London: HM Stationery Office, 1959).

ACCIDENTALS

p. 205, *Daniel Dennett, a consciousness theorist, famously said*: Daniel Dennett, *Consciousness Explained* (Boston: Little Brown, 1991).

p. 206, *Albert Einstein, on his deathbed*: This Einstein quote is well reported; the deathbed scene, however, could be apocryphal.

p. 212, *("Mental representations, or memes . . .":* Preti and Miotto, "Creativity, Evolution and Mental Illnesses."

LANGUAGE GARDEN

p. 225, *Or you could argue, with linguist Derek Bickerton*: Derek Bickerton, *Language and Species* (Chicago: University of Chicago Press, 1990).

p. 228, *Merlin Donald wails*: Donald, *A Mind So Rare*.

ACKNOWLEDGMENTS

In writing a book like this one, I feel I become almost a conduit, a listener who produces something perhaps of value only insofar as something of value is given by those generous enough to share their insight or their stories. In this I have been rich. And I turn to the business of writing acknowledgments last, and slowly, because what I owe to others is enormous. I would almost rather you read this than read the book.

For the generosity of Drs. William Calvin and Freeman Dyson in answering my questions, thank you. Thanks to philosopher Todd Moody, for a lively e-mail exchange. *Mille grazie* to Dr. Antonio Preti, who has taken time out of his schedule to answer my questions comprehensively and *spiritosamente,* and who led me on to many other invaluable sources. Thank you, Jim Nollman, for your insight into the minds of your companions, the whales. And much gratitude to Lyn Miles, for allowing me to tag along with you and Chantek, your gallant red-haired child. Thanks to Ken Quinn, court reporter here in Whatcom County, Washington, a generous resource.

Robert Hass, I offer much appreciation for your words, which have been a gift: both those words offered in person and those you have written.

To my colleague Ned Markosian, thank you for a cup of coffee that helped frame some complicated thoughts.

Within the world of neurodiversity on the Web, two very important sites belong to Kathleen Seidel and my friend Suz, from England; both represent very important voices in the field of neurodiversity and autism. Both responded to my questions with pages of carefully thought-through, challenging, and articulate response, for which I give in return my necessarily brief but deep thanks.

Thanks to *Orion* magazine and *Biography,* where chapters of this book, in altered form, originally appeared. Special thanks to Aina Barton at *Orion,* a wise and generous editor.

Among my friends, I am grateful to Penny Chambers and Rosina Lippi, who provided clarifying moments they have generously let me use in these pages. Thank you, Mary Janell Metzger, for your humor and your constant support. Many obeisances of the page to Brenda Miller, for your help with this book and for your friendship.

Thank you, thank you, Thor Hansen, the muse of Victor Street.

For my family at St. Nicholas Orthodox Church, love and thanks. Blessings to Susan Bennerstrom and David Scherrer, for the gifts of art and photography and your love and your kindness. Thanks to Lee Gulyas and Ed Gulyas, spiritual and culinary guides, and of course, dear Fia. Thanks to Father Joe, for his time and thoughtfulness.

To Dawn Prince-Hughes, you have been a part of this since my first ventures into the subject—part of the shaping of the subject—and a beloved friend. You have been unstintingly generous in allowing me to use your experiences, and I breathe your love and support like air.

And to N'Lili and Olivia, it is hard to express the generosity and courage you showed as you allowed me to look into your lives freely and openly, understanding that for me writing is intimately connected with loving. In the real world and in cyberspace, I always think about you, with arms out and with love.

Jill Grinberg, someone I completely trust, your guidance enables me to feel my way along the most difficult subjects. Beyond that, your encouragement means the world to me; you have more faith in me, I think, than I have in myself. I don't want to use the formula "I thank my agent"; you are truly my friend.

To Sara Carder at Tarcher/Penguin, you have guided me through this book throughout its composition with intelligence, compassion, and the kind of editorial imagination that's precious in its scarcity. I claim my own flaws, but this book would not exist without you.

To Bruce Beasley, you are my first best reader, my life's *amor*, my kibitzer, the one who feeds my body and spirit with the most luscious ideas and the smartest biscuits and much more than I can express. This is my beloved, and this is my friend.

To my son, Jin. For your Pokémon and Silly Sandwiches, the beauty of your heart and mind, the way you cried when you stepped on a fly, your potato-bug day care, your stomping feet, all of you. In words you invented, I love you so much I can't explain.

ABOUT THE AUTHOR

Susanne Antonetta's *Body Toxic: An Environmental Memoir* (Counterpoint, 2001) was described in *The New York Times* as "a considerable achievement" that has "posed a challenge to our prevailing notions of science and journalism and even literary narrative." In 2001, *Body Toxic* went on to become a New York Times Notable Book and to place on many other book-of-the-year lists, including Amazon's Top Ten Memoirs. *Body Toxic* won a 2001 American Book Award. Antonetta's four books of poetry include *The Lives of the Saints* (University of Washington Press, 2002)—a finalist for the Lenore Marshall award—and *Bardo* (University of Wisconsin Press, 1998), winner of the Brittingham Prize. She is the recipient of an Artist Trust grant from Washington State for poetry, and a National Endowment for the Arts grant for nonfiction. She lives on the shores of Puget Sound, in Washington, with her husband and son.